RA COTTERILL

GW00707826

Longman Exam Guides
Monetary Economics

Longman Exam Guides

Series Editors: **Stuart Wall and David Weigall**

Titles available:

Bookkeeping and Accounting
Business Law
Economics
English as a Foreign Language
English Literature
Monetary Economics
Office Practice and Secretarial Administration
Pure Mathematics
Secretarial Skills

Forthcoming:

Biology
Business Communication
Business Studies
Chemistry
Commerce
Computer Science
Electronics
French
General Principles of Law
General Studies
Geography
Mechanics
Modern British History
Physics
Politics
Principles of Law
Quantitive Methods
Sociology
Taxation

Longman Exam Guides

MONETARY ECONOMICS

B. Julian Beecham

LONGMAN
London and New York

Longman Group Limited
Longman House, Burnt Mill, Harlow
Essex CM20 2JE, England
Associated companies throughout the world

*Published in the United States of America
by Longman Inc., New York*

© Longman Group Limited 1986

All rights reserved; no part of this publication may be
reproduced, stored in a retrieval system, or transmitted
in any form or by any means, electronic, mechanical,
photocopying, recording, or otherwise, without the
prior written permission of the Publishers.

First published 1986

British Library Cataloguing in Publication Data
Beecham, B. Julian
  Monetary economics.——
  (Longman exam guides)
  1. Money
  I. Title
  332.4   HG221

ISBN 0-582-29683-8

Library of Congress Cataloging in Publication Data
Beecham, B. Julian, 1927–
  Monetary economics
  (Longman exam guides)
  Includes index.
  1. Money.   2. Monetary policy.   3. International
finance. I. Title. II. Series
HG221.B424 1986   332.4   85–23992
ISBN 0-582-29683-8

Set in 9½ on 11pt Linotron Times
by The Word Factory Ltd, Rossendale, Lancs.
Printed and Bound in Great Britain at
The Bath Press, Avon

Contents

Editors' Preface

Much has been said in recent years about declining standards and disappointing examination results. While this may be somewhat exaggerated, examiners are well aware that the performance of many candidates falls well short of their potential. *Longman Exam Guides* are written by experienced examiners and teachers, and aim to give you the best possible foundation for examination success. There is no attempt to cut corners. The books encourage thorough study and a full understanding of the concepts involved and should be seen as course companions and study guides to be used throughout the year. Examiners are in no doubt that a structured approach in preparing for and taking examinations can, together with hard work and diligent application, substantially improve performance.

The largely self-contained nature of each chapter gives the book a useful degree of flexibility. After starting with Chapters 1 and 2, all other chapters can be read selectively, in any order appropriate to the stage you have reached in your course. We believe that this book, and the series as a whole, will help you establish a solid platform of basic knowledge and examination technique on which to build.

Stuart Wall and David Weigall

Introduction

This book has been designed as the most direct route to meeting the requirements of the Monetary Economics examination paper of The Institute of Bankers.

Chapter 1 provides pointers on how best to use your private study time in preparing for the examination. It also gives suggestions on examination technique, i.e. on how you actually conduct yourself during the examination itself. Adherence to both should help you to achieve success in the examinations you take.

Chapters 2 to 9 are arranged in sequence with the layout of the current Monetary Economics syllabus. Each chapter begins by stating the requirements of the syllabus for the topic covered in that chapter. This is followed by a section which briefly defines the technical terms involved and which gives an overview of the topic area in question, to help you get started. Then follow two sections dealing with the essential theories and principles connected with the topic; one dealing with their explanation and the other with their application to the UK Monetary Economics scene. These sections are backed up by six examination questions recently set in that topic area, together with outline answers. There then follows a full specimen answer to a carefully chosen recent examination question: this is to help you improve your technique in how best to answer a question, the whole question and nothing but the question. Finally, each chapter ends with advice on how to take a step further in keeping yourself fully abreast of movements in the subject matter of each topic.

Since the 1982 changes in the Monetary Economics syllabus, the general thrust of the examination has been modified. The questions asked are rather more direct, seeking precise up-to-date information and understanding – that is what makes them difficult for those candidates who have generally learned financial archaeology, instead of concentrating on acquiring a finely focused perspective of the evolving subject matter of Monetary Economics.

Acknowledgements

My grateful thanks to:

Nick Douch for his constructive criticism and advice which kept me on the 'straight and narrow'.

The Institute of Bankers, and Alan Davies, for their generous permission to use the Monetary Economics *Examiners' Reports*, Monetary Economics *Syllabus*, *Updating Notes* and Waterlow Publishers Ltd for permission to use some articles from *Banking World*.

Banking Information Service for kind permission to draw from their excellent publications: *A Guide to Monetary Economics*; *A Guide to the British Financial System*; and *A Guide to the International Financial System*;

The Bank of England for permission to refer to two articles in their *Quarterly Bulletins*, and *Financial Times* for allowing the use of their London Money Market Rates table;

And to Enid, my wife, for tidying and typing the manuscript with great efficiency.

B. Julian Beecham
Cardiff
Jan 1986

To my students

Chapter 1

Study and examination techniques

If you know where you're going, you're halfway there.

A careful use of your private study time in preparation for the examination, and a well-practised examination technique, are perhaps the two most important requirements for examination 'success'.

PREPARATION

1. Make sure that you fully know, and have in your possession, the latest IOB syllabus for Monetary Economics.
2. Create study time within your weekly activities. Discipline yourself to stick to the study time. Within the study time allocate time to *all* subjects within the course you are studying. Set study targets and endeavour to achieve them so that you cover the whole syllabus. This last point is even more important where students are taking examinations by correspondence course and by private study.
3. Read as much as you can around each topic from the quality daily and weekly newspapers, banking magazines and other learned journals and bulletins. Watch and listen to appropriate programmes on the television and radio. These activities will help you to update your knowledge and to understand technical terms more fully. They will also help you appreciate the context in which to place your essays, assignments and answers to examination questions.
4. When you come to write essays or assignments, you should first collect all the relevant data and information from the references suggested by your tutors. Make good use of the college and public libraries. Your opening paragraph should clearly state what the scope of the essay/assignment is and how you intend to meet it. It is extremely helpful to make an answer plan, in which you identify the main points to be raised. Arrange these points *before* you begin to write the essay/assignment: this will give your

essay a clear structure. Write one paragraph on each point, using headings if you feel this makes the answer clearer. Keep a dictionary handy to avoid spelling mistakes. Also avoid bad grammar, emotive language and unnecessary repetition. Wherever appropriate bring the points you have made together in a conclusion. Remember to answer the question, the whole question and nothing but the question!

5. Where chief examiners' and moderators' reports are available, study them carefully to find out which topics usually cause most problems and why!

6. Read any article that the examiner might write about the subject.

7. Design your overall study programme in such a way that you leave time for revision before the examinations.

EXAMINATION TECHNIQUE

1. In the examination room, read the question paper through and spend five to ten minutes deciding which questions you are going to answer. Use time too to make sure you understand exactly what the examiner is asking.

2. Allocate your time to the required number of questions.

3. Tackle first the question which you can answer best – build up confidence.

4. Plan your answer by setting down the main points and arranging them in their logical order *before* beginning to write in detail.

5. Be brief and relevant – you will get no marks for irrelevant material, however well it is expressed.

6. If there is more than one part to a question, make sure you answer all parts.

7. Answer the right number of questions. If you are required to answer four, then the examiner will mark the first four you have done and will ignore anything else.

8. Finally, read what you have written, correct as necessary, and cut out anything which does not make sense.

OVERALL

Remember, this is not a subject you can memorize or swot; it is one that requires understanding which can be obtained only by application throughout the course. Last-minute revision alone almost certainly spells disaster.

Chapter 2

Money

- Revise the nature, types and functions of money and the problems encountered in defining money.
- Identify the concept of liquidity and distinguish between 'money' and other financial assets.
- Be aware of the RPI and TPI measurements of the value of money and of the problems of money fulfilling its functions during a period of instability (including a mention of index linking of financial assets).
- Measure and analyse the composition of the money stock, assessing the differences between the various monetary aggregates which may be used for control purposes.

GETTING STARTED

ORIGIN OF MONEY

The one main characteristic which separates man from other animals is his continuing dissatisfaction with the present state of his material well-being. Even the most primitive man realized two things:

1. On his own he could not produce all that was needed to improve his material welfare.
2. The best way to get the goods he needed, but could not produce, was by creating a surplus of those goods which he could produce best, and then exchanging his surplus for the specialized surpluses of others.

   The realization of these two things led man away from 'direct production' (consuming whatever he could produce entirely by himself) to 'indirect production' (swapping his surplus produce for that of others and thus satisfying many more wants). Adoption of indirect production or *barter* as the way of life led human beings to accept division of labour and the consequent specialization of production; this changed man from being an independent unit into an interdependent part of the community.

Division of labour and specialization presuppose *exchange*. The method of exchange practised by primitive man was barter (direct swap of specialized surpluses): if A had surplus wheat but lacked spears, he could try and find, say, B who had surplus spears and, at the same time, needed wheat. Since both A and B wanted each other's surplus products, the direct swap, after some haggling, took place.

Barter was better than no exchange because it raised the living standard of the community above the subsistence level of existence. However primitive man soon realized that barter, too, was clumsy in at least three respects:

1. While A may desperately want B's spears, B may not want A's wheat in exchange at that particular time. This lack of a double coincidence of wants made barter very awkward.
2. The barter system came unstuck when small transactions were involved. Suppose C needed wheat and had a surplus ox which he was willing to exchange for, say, 100 bags of wheat; and that A wanted the ox but had only 20 bags of wheat to spare. In this case there was clearly a lack of small change for small transactions.
3. There was the problem of the rate of exchange: how much wheat should A give for how many of B's spears? The term 'barter' comes from Old French 'barater', meaning 'to cheat': how much wheat was given in exchange for how many spears depended largely upon who, between A and B, was the more persuasive and cunning.

Man's growing dissatisfaction with exchange under barter led him to evolve a less direct system of exchange, i.e. exchanging surpluses for one *generally acceptable* 'commodity', and using the stores of that 'commodity' in exchange for whatever goods were needed. Since all goods were exchangeable for the 'commodity', the 'commodity' itself became the means of exchange. From cowrie shells in India to pressed cubes of tea in China, from furs in Persia to cattle in Greece – all these commodities have acted as the means of exchange in earlier times in these ancient civilizations.

The clues to the evolution of 'money' in Western civilizations are found in the usage of cattle by the Greeks as the means of exchange. The ancient Greeks used cattle as 'money'. The Latin word 'pecus' means 'a single head of cattle', and *pecus* is also the root of the English word 'pecuniary', meaning 'relating to wealth and property', and 'pecunia', which comes from *pecus*, means 'money'. There is a close link between the evolution of money in the western world and the use of cattle as money by the ancient Greeks. The sequence most commonly put forward for the evolution of money goes like this: first there was no trade, then there was barter – and a little trade, then there was money – and plenty of trade.

ESSENTIAL PRINCIPLES

CHARACTERISTICS OF MONEY

During the course of the evolution of money, certain attributes or characteristics came to be expected from the commodity acting as money or the means of exchange.

1. *Acceptability*: it should be generally accepted by virtue of its intrinsic value; if not because of that, then by decree, convention or convenience.
2. *Scarcity*: to be scarce, its supply should remain less than its demand; but it should not be too scarce, otherwise it would be hoarded and would not circulate freely. Essentially its supply must in some way be controlled.
3. *Recognizability*: in order to avoid unfair practices.
4. *Divisibility*: it should be capable of being divided into small units without loss of value.
5. *Stability*: the conditions of its supply and demand should remain stable so that its 'value' remains stable – i.e. what it obtains today in exchange, it obtained in the past and would obtain in the future.
6. *Homogeneity*: each of its units should be exactly the same as every other unit; otherwise people would hold on to the more valuable units and would release the less valuable units, thereby destabilizing its supply and demand conditions.
7. *Portability*: each unit should have small weight and bulk compared to its value, so that it could be easily carried about.
8. *Durability*: it should not be a wasting asset, either physically or in terms of its value; no one wants to hold on to a wasting asset.

FUNCTIONS OF MONEY

The commodity which possessed the above characteristics could perform at once the *functions* of money, viz.:

1. *Act as the medium of exchange*: it should split exchange, first, into a process of sale of one's goods and services for money, and second, into a process of purchase of the goods and services wanted in exchange. It should act as wealth with liquid purchasing power, giving its possessor the freedom of choice in the satisfaction of wants, and enabling him to save and lend easily.
2. *Unit of account or standard of value*: it measures the values of all other things because they are exchanged for it. 'Price' is the value of a good in terms of money; by comparing the prices of various goods their values can be compared. As the unit of account, it enables accounts to be kept, costs to be assessed precisely and choices to be made between competing projects by comparing the costs and returns from each.
3. *Store of value*: it enables wealth to be stored up indefinitely without deterioration in value. It can then be exchanged, now and in the future, without loss in purchasing power, for other goods.
4. *Standard for deferred payments*: it enables contracts to be fulfilled in the future to be assessed now, thereby equating present and future values. The equation of present and future

values is crucial to lenders making loans to borrowers who contract to repay an agreed sum regularly over several months or even years.

A commodity which does not possess the attributes of money cannot perform all the functions of money. However, it is important to note that while the attributes and the functions of money are closely connected, they are *not* synonymous.

FORMS OF MONEY

To have a proper concept of money one must know at least two things about money. First, the precise attributes the commodity must possess in order to perform the functions of money. Second, the particular commodities which have at different times acted as money.

Precious metals and coins

Precious metals ultimately came to be accepted as more satisfactory than cattle, etc. in acting as money; they were always in demand for ornaments and decorations, were in continuous but restricted supply, were recognizable, had a high and stable value, and could be divided into small units without loss of value. Above all, they were readily and generally acceptable. Initially, precious metals had to be carried about in bulk along with a pair of scales so that the exact quantity to be used for each purchase could be weighed. When coins of various values were minted by the monetary authorities, the weight of the metal in each coin was guaranteed by the issuing authority by the imprint of the ruler's seal. Unfortunately, some people, for personal gain, resorted to 'clipping' the coins, i.e. cutting small pieces off the edges of gold coins. To prevent clipping, coins were issued with milled edges.

The link between 'coins' and 'money' is interesting, and it lies in the Latin word 'moneta', which was a surname for the Roman goddess Juno. Roman money was made from precious metals in the temple of Juno Moneta, and Moneta came to be known as 'mint', a place where money was coined or minted. The Romans stamped the effigy of an ox on the metal tokens because cattle were used as money. From the Latin 'moneta' came the Old French word 'monnie', which gave birth to the English word 'money'.

There are two types of coins: standard and token. In a *standard coin*, the value of the metal in the coin is equivalent to its face value, i.e. the value embossed upon it by the issuing authority. The value of metal contained in a *token coin* is less than its face value. People accept token coins by decree and because they have confidence in the issuing authority. Token coins came into being because the supply of precious metals began to fall short of demand. Precious metals were now needed to finance the rapidly increasing trade due to the introduction of a money system of exchange.

Paper money

To economize on the usage of precious metals and to avoid carrying heavy and bulky coins about, paper money came into use. Paper money can be *convertible*, i.e. it can be exchanged, on demand, into precious metals (gold or silver); or it can be *inconvertible*, i.e. it cannot be exchanged into precious metals or into any other form of money at full face value. Inconvertible paper money is generally *fiduciary money*, i.e. not backed by gold. It is issued 'in trust', and is usually backed by some form of government debt.

Bank deposits

In countries where banking and financial systems are not developed, coins and paper money (bank notes) form the major proportion of their total money supply. In countries with highly developed banking systems, deposits with banks and other financial institutions are also an important component of the money supply. The *sight* bank deposits are deposits which can be withdrawn on demand, either in part or in full. Sight or demand deposits are clearly money since they possess the major characteristics of money, being generally acceptable, divisible and transferable by cheque; they also perform all the functions of money.

Near money

There are financial assets which closely resemble money but which lack the general acceptability of money; i.e. they have to be converted into real money (notes and coins or demand deposit balances) before they can be used as money. This conversion process may involve inconvenience, delay or risk of loss in monetary value. These financial assets are known as 'quasi' or 'near' money. Bank seven-day deposits and most building society term deposits are a good example of near money. Building society share deposits are traditionally thought of as 'near money' because cheques cannot be written directly on the account. However, withdrawals can now be made instantaneously without loss of interest and even on a Saturday! Although purists would argue about the absence of cheques, the distinction is now more blurred.

The near money assets have two functions:

1. To earn interest and to act as a store of wealth. Thus they are attractive to those who are able to save. In most cases, real money yields no interest and therefore, unlike near money, provides no hedge against inflation.
2. To be fairly quickly convertible into cash, without significant risk of loss, either of interest or of capital. It may therefore be attractive to plan to make larger payments out of near money assets rather than out of real money.

The technical definition of 'liquidity' separates real money from near money: real money *is* liquid purchasing power and can be directly exchanged for goods and services, whereas near money is *not* liquid purchasing power. If near money is to be used directly to purchase goods and services, it must first be converted into cash; this requirement of conversion into cash, with the consequent risk of monetary loss, differentiates near money assets from real money.

LIQUIDITY SPECTRUM

It is absolutely essential to understand that the concept of money is very closely linked with the concept of liquidity. A liquid asset is one that can be easily turned into cash without the risk of loss. On the one extreme of the liquidity spectrum we have real money with instant liquid purchasing power. In the middle we have near money assets which have a definite money value but which do not directly function as a medium of exchange. On the other extreme, we have 'non-money', i.e. physical assets which are least liquid in their ability to act as a medium of exchange, e.g. houses, or fixed long-term bonds. In the liquidity spectrum, it would be wrong to draw absolute dividing lines between various types of money and other financial assets because there *is* substitutability, especially at the margin, between various types of money and specified financial assets. The more complex, sophisticated and stable the financial institutions a country has, the greater the variety of financial assets available to the public and the greater the degree of substitutability there is likely to be among these financial assets.

THE VALUE OF MONEY

The value of money is its purchasing power, i.e. the goods and services it obtains through exchange. Therefore a fall in the value of money is the same thing as a general rise in prices and *vice versa*. Thus the value of money changes inversely with changes in the general price level.

INDEX NUMBERS AND THE VALUE OF MONEY

In most countries the changes in the value of money are measured by a number of statistical devices, known as *index numbers*. These attempt to measure changes in the purchasing power of money over given periods. The following are among the more-used indices.

Consumer price index (CPI)

This is used in the United States of America. It is constructed from the retail prices of about 400 goods and services widely sold in the country. Each product in the CPI is weighted by its importance in the individual consumer's budget, i.e. by its share in the total dollar value of the individual consumer's purchases. The current prices are compared to those of a selected base year by expressing the current prices as a percentage of prices in the base year. Since the value of money is its purchasing power, the CPI, by comparing current purchasing power with that in the base year, indicates the changes which have taken place in the value of money. Changes in the CPI, in turn, suggest changes in the real value of money incomes.

The CPI however, has two major drawbacks in this respect: first, its difficulty in assessing changes in the quality of goods purchased now and in the base year. For example, it is difficult to compare the current prices of, say, television sets with those of 10 or 15 years ago, because this product, like many others, has been considerably improved over the years. This improvement is partly reflected in the current higher prices which may not, therefore, reflect a 'true' fall in the real value of money incomes. Second, its difficulty in assessing the effects of changes in tastes or demand. Higher prices may, in part, reflect an increased preference by society for certain goods and services, resulting in increased demand, rather than a fall in the real value of money incomes.

Retail price index (RPI)	This is the UK equivalent of the American CPI, and is constructed largely according to the principles of the CPI. The RPI is commonly used in the UK to measure changes in the value of money, and therefore real incomes, over a given period. It is based on a 'basket of goods' which are seen as reflecting average expenditure patterns in UK households. If the purchase price of the basket in a given month is, say, 10 per cent higher than on the base date, then it is assumed by the public, trade unions, employers and the government that the value of money in the UK has fallen by 10 per cent; the same sum of money buys 10 per cent less now than it did on the base date. Such a general assumption can be misleading. Large groups of the population will have different expenditure patterns and may not be fully affected by changes in the prices of the goods in the basket. For example, a rise in mortgage rates or 'motor tax' will not affect those with no mortgage debt or motor cars. Consumption patterns change at different levels of income or with individual tastes.
Wholesale price index (WPI)	This measures changes in the wholesale prices of a number of representative commodities, ranging from raw materials to finished goods. Like all other indices, it too 'weights' products, compares their prices to those of a given base year, and expresses the current prices as a percentage of prices in the base year in order to show changes in the value of money. The drawback with the WPI is that the prices are list prices quoted by manufacturers (i.e. wholesale prices) rather than current prices at which the commodities are actually traded (i.e. retail prices).
Tax and price index (TPI)	This index number, devised in 1979, attempts to show how changes in prices *and* in direct taxes affect the purchasing power of incomes. For example, an increase in indirect taxes and a decrease in direct taxes may leave people just as they were in their purchasing capacities: people may pay more for goods and services because of an increase in the indirect tax on goods and services, but have more money after a decrease in income tax to pay for them. The present government assumes that the TPI is more reliable in determining the purchasing power of individuals than the RPI. The major drawback of the TPI is that it ignores the effects of changes in the indirect and direct taxation rates upon those whose incomes are *below* the income tax threshold; they will have to pay more for goods and services *without* being compensated by cuts in income tax rates.

One important point to note in connection with all index numbers is that all price indices suffer from statistical errors, imprecision and misrepresentation. Due to these drawbacks, changes in the value of money cannot be measured precisely. It is useful to be fully aware of this fact.

THEORIES OF THE VALUE OF MONEY

There are several theories of the value of money; however, the following have become the more important because of the preoccupation of most governments with controlling the money supply in order to maintain the real value of money.

The quantity theory of money (QTM)

This theory states that the level of spending and prices is directly proportional to the amount of money in circulation. Thus an increase in money in circulation will raise spending and prices; whereas a decrease in money in circulation will lower spending and prices.

Basically the quantity theory assumes that prices are always proportional to total spending, and that total spending is always proportional to the total stock of money in circulation. Neither of these assumptions, however, is necessarily valid: first, a more efficient method of production may increase output with little, or even no, increase in production costs; therefore the producer may be able to raise his output to meet an increase in total spending on his product with little, or even no increase in prices. Prices need not, therefore, be proportional to total spending. Second, total spending represents a flow of incomes over time, and can vary *independently* of the stock of money in circulation. For example, total spending would be affected by a change in the *velocity* at which a given stock of money circulates within the economy. Total spending need not, therefore, be proportional to the total stock of money in circulation.

The quantity equation

This is a mathematical expression of QTM which takes explicit account of the velocity of money in circulation.
According to this equation, $MV = PT$, where

> M = quantity of money (cash and chequeable accounts)
> V = velocity of circulation (the rate of turnover of M)
> P = general price level (or a price index, say, RPI)
> T = total number of transactions (total real output)

The equation states that total spending (MV) is always equal to total receipts (PT). Since the equation must be true by definition, it is not a theory but a truism; a theory must explain what causes the value of money to change. The Quantity equation simply states that $P = MV/T$, i.e. that the value of money increases (P-falls) if the same total spending (MV) buys *more* real goods and services (T); and that the value of money falls (i.e. P rises) when the money supply (M) increases or when its velocity of circulation (V) becomes faster, with total real output (T) remaining unchanged.

Since the equation is true by definition, it can be used to *predict* changes in the money value of real output only if the speed with which people spend money balances (V) tends to remain constant. Under full employment of labour and capacity in an economy, the real output would be relatively stable. Only in this special case could the equation be used to predict that an increase in money supply will cause a proportional upward change in prices.

During the upswing of the economy, when prices are rising, an expansion of bank credit may increase money supply; this would be the exact opposite of the QTM or its mathematical expression. In this case the increase in the money supply is the result, rather than the cause, of rising prices. QTM is a *supply*-based theory; as such it pays insufficient attention to the *demand* for money, which is governed by the need of individuals and firms to hold ready cash for current requirements or to meet emergencies, and to hold cash in order to make capital gains (buying bonds when the interest rate is high and selling them when it is low. See Ch. 6). Changes in demand are reflected in changes in V and, as we have seen, when V changes the QTM loses all powers of prediction.

INFLATION, DEFLATION AND THE VALUE OF MONEY

The phenomena of *inflation* and *deflation* cause changes in the value of money.

The outward sign of *inflation* in an economy is an increase in the general price level. But the reason for a rise in prices is increased total spending relative to the supply of goods and services on sale: too much money chasing too few goods and services. The net result of inflation on the value of money is to decrease the purchasing power of money.

There are four major causes of inflation.

1. High demand for bank loans which, when granted and spent, increase money supply (see Ch. 4). The resulting increase in demand pulls up the prices of consumer and capital goods. This in turn increases the demand for more bank loans, which pulls up prices still more. The cause of this type of inflation is *demand pull*. Demand pull can also be triggered by a sharp and significant rise in the demand for exports, with the result that too much money is chasing too few goods in the domestic economy.
2. Heavy government spending to reflate the economy, in order to bring it out of deep recession, can also create inflation: prices will rise until increased output matches increased aggregate demand.
3. A successful and continuous demand for higher wages will cause businessmen to raise prices continuously in order to recoup their higher labour costs. The rise in prices then triggers off demand for still higher wages. This cause of inflation is called *cost push*: prices are pushed up, at least initially, by higher labour costs.
4. An inflationary psychology which motivates people to spend savings quickly in order to avoid a further decline in the purchasing power of their money. This will increase the general price level, owing to increased total spending relative to the goods and services available in the market.

Deflation is a phenomenon which causes a decrease in the general price level, due to a decrease in total spending relative to the supply of goods and services on the market. Deflation increases the value of money i.e. its purchasing power. It benefits those on fixed incomes and creditors. It causes businesses to decline, unemployment to rise and incomes to fall. Deflation has not really occurred in Britain since the 1930s.

LEGAL TENDER

While money is something which people will generally accept in settlement of debts, legal tender is what the law says they must accept if it is offered. Legal tender may be *limited* legal tender, i.e. people must accept it if offered, but only up to specified limits of payment; on the other hand it may be *unlimited* legal tender, i.e. it must be accepted in settlement of debts of any amount.

USEFUL APPLIED MATERIALS

LEGAL TENDER IN BRITAIN

The legal tender in Britain consists of Bank of England notes and the coins minted at the Royal Mint. The Bank of England notes, issued in various denominations, are *unlimited* legal tender in the UK. Scottish and Northern Irish bank notes are not legal tender in England and Wales but are *unlimited* legal tender in Scotland and Northern Ireland. The one pound coin, minted at the Royal Mint, is also *unlimited* legal tender. Other coins minted at the Royal Mint are *limited* legal tender in the UK; debts of up to £10 can be paid in 50p coins; of up to £5 by other cupro-nickel coins, and up to 20p by bronze coins. All coins are token coins.

The development of bank notes is an important area of study, so that a brief account is given here. In the seventeenth century, gold was stored with the London goldsmiths for safe-keeping, and withdrawals were allowed when required. The goldsmiths gave the depositors receipts for the gold stored. These receipts were negotiable as total or partial payments for purchases, by 'endorsement', i.e. by the owner signing at the back of the receipt; this practice avoided the physical handling of gold and the risk of robbery. The goldsmiths' receipts were promissory notes, promising to pay on demand the stated amount of gold; they were backed by gold in the safes of the issuing goldsmith and were readily convertible. Thus these receipts became in effect paper money. The lending operations of the goldsmiths were facilitated by issuing receipts in round sums, payable to the bearer on demand. In the nineteenth century, country banks emerged and issued their own notes backed by their own reserves, and the Bank of England (founded in 1694 – see Ch. 3) issued noted backed by the UK gold reserves. In 1931, the gold backing was withdrawn almost completely, so that the Bank of England notes became *fiduciary* and inconvertible. At present, the Bank of England is the sole note-issuing authority in England and Wales. However, Scottish and Northern Irish banks also issue notes with certain restrictions (see Ch. 5). The total of notes and coins is often colloquially referred to as the 'cash'.

BANK DEPOSITS

The chequeable sight deposits in Britain, as in other countries with highly developed banking systems, are an important feature of the money in the economy. The medium of exchange in Britain consists of notes and coins and chequeable current accounts. In the not too distant future, the leading building societies will probably also provide full chequeing accounts payable on demand which will therefore have to be regarded as money.

The *near money* assets in Britain include postal orders, money orders, bills of exchange, building society deposits, national savings securities, Treasury bills, local authority deposits, certificates of tax deposit (for the corporation tax paid in advance by business companies), certificates of deposit (sold by banks to large depositors), and National Savings accounts.

OFFICIAL MONETARY AGGREGATES IN BRITAIN

The meaning, measurement and control of money are inter-related concepts. If the monetary authorities (the Treasury and the Bank of England) do not know precisely what money is, and what forms it can take, then they will not be able to measure it, nor will they be able to control its supply.

In Britain today, there are *seven* monetary and liquidity aggregates. In order to understand why there are so many official definitions of money, you must first and foremost understand the concept of the liquidity spectrum (see p. 8). The various aggregates differ in their composition and in their response to changes in interest rates, incomes and inflation.

In Britain, as in most other countries, a distinction is made between 'narrow' and 'broad' measures of money. The *narrow* money measures include those assets which represent immediate purchasing power, i.e. those assets which perform the medium of exchange function of money. Narrow money comprising *immediately* available purchasing power might well understate the *potential* purchasing power in the economy, given the existence of liquid assets which could quickly, and without significant financial loss, be converted into cash; hence the need for *broad* money measures.

Until 1982, there were in Britain three monetary (M) aggregates, and two private sector liquidity measures (PSLs). The components of these aggregates and measures were:

1. **M1** = notes and coins in circulation with the public *plus* sterling sight bank deposits of the private sector. M1 represented the sum of *narrow money* in the economy, i.e. the total immediate purchasing power.
2. **Sterling M3** = M1 *plus* private sector sterling time bank deposits *plus* private sector holdings of sterling certificates of deposit, *plus* public sector sterling sight and time deposits (certificates of deposits are receipts issued by banks for sums of money deposited with them for a fixed period of time; they are easily negotiable). Sterling M3 represented the sum of *broad money*, in sterling only, in the economy. Since 1984 public sector deposits have been excluded from this definition (see below).
3. **M3** = Sterling M3 *plus* foreign currency bank deposits of the UK private and public sectors. M3 represented the broadest definition of *money stock* in the UK economy (see below).

Another way to look at money stock is to measure changes in the amount of liquid assets held by the private sector (excluding banks) which it can use for consumption or investment immediately or at short notice. The measures of the private sector liquidity in the UK were:

4. **PSL1** = M1 *plus* private sector holdings of sterling time deposits with up to two years to maturity, *plus* sterling certificates of deposit, *plus* other money market financial instruments, *plus* certificates of tax deposits (these certificates are receipts of tax paid in advance). The connections between monetary aggregates M1 and sterling M3 and PSL1 are obvious: M1 is a component of PSL1 and private sector holdings of sterling time deposits and sterling certificates of deposit are included in sterling M3 and PSL1.

5. **PSL2** = PSL1 *plus* private sector holdings of building society deposits (excluding term shares and SAYE contracts, both of which are not liquid), *plus* National Savings securities (excluding National Savings SAYE contracts and other long-term deposits which are not liquid) *minus* building society holdings of bank deposits and money market instruments (to avoid double-counting).

The purpose of measuring PSL1 and PSL2 is to gauge the changes in economic behaviour associated with a change in holdings of liquid assets. The reason why PSL1 and PSL2 measures are needed in addition to monetary aggregates is that the monetary aggregates do *not* include liquid assets in the shape of building society deposits, National Savings securities and certificates of tax deposits, because these assets are not traditionally regarded as money. The PSL1 and PSL2 liquidity aggregates are themselves regarded as *broad* measures.

The purpose in measuring monetary and liquidity aggregates is to discover by how much and how rapidly the money supply is rising, and from this to predict future changes in economic activity.

CHANGES IN MONETARY AGGREGATES SINCE 1982

Until 1982, the M1 aggregate, i.e. notes and coins in circulation with the public, and the sterling non-interest bearing bank sight deposits of the private sector, provided a reasonably clear measure of immediate purchasing power, i.e. *narrow money*. In recent years, however, M1 has included a growing element of *interest-bearing* sight deposits. These deposits mainly represent volatile overnight deposits of large corporations and institutions in the form of investment funds, rather than money to be spent on goods and services. Thus M1, as traditionally defined, began to misrepresent the concept of 'immediately available purchasing power'. Furthermore, the components of M1 did not include those deposits in banks, building societies and National Savings Bank ordinary accounts which are more or less instantly available for making purchases (near money deposits). The inability of M1 to represent the sum total of immediate purchasing power led the monetary authorities to introduce a new monetary aggregate, M2, in 1982.

M2

M2 includes all those assets which might legitimately be regarded as the 'transaction balances' of the private sector. The authorities define the M2 aggregate as the sum total of 'notes and coins in circulation with the public, *plus* sterling *retail* deposits held by the UK private sector with the UK monetary sector, with building societies and in the National Savings Bank ordinary account'.

Sterling retail deposits include:

1. All non-interest bearing sight deposits.
2. All other deposits (regardless of size and maturity) on which cheques may be drawn or from which standing orders, direct debit mandates or other payments to third parties may be made.
3. Other deposits of less than £100,000 having a maturity of less than one month. Deposits of £100,000 and over, or with maturities over one month are held mainly as investment and are therefore not sufficiently liquid.
4. All shares and deposits with building societies which are within one month of maturity.
5. All deposits with the National Savings Bank ordinary account.

The monetary logic underlying the introduction of M2 is to provide a monetary aggregate that comprises the 'transaction' balances of the private sector in modern times, an aggregate which is neither so narrow as to be confined to notes and coins and current accounts, nor so broad as to include large investment balances.

M0

In October 1983, the authorities unveiled the newest monetary aggregate, **M0**. M0 includes notes and coins in circulation with the public, *plus* till money of banks, *plus* bankers' operational balances with the Bank of England. The rationale for its introduction is principally the same as for the introduction of M2: i.e. that M1 now includes 25 per cent of interest-bearing sight deposits which are *not* transaction deposits but rather investment deposits. M0 further emphasizes the distinction which the authorities have drawn between, on the one hand, 'narrow' money or transaction balances, which they believe respond unambiguously and consistently to changes in short-term interest rates, and, on the other hand, 'broad' money, or private sector liquidity, which has particular relevance for decisions about fiscal and funding policies – these official policies relate to tax revenue, public spending and borrowing activities.

In the Budget of 1984 it was confirmed that, for the period February 1984 to April 1985, target ranges for monetary growth would apply to the aggregates M0 (narrow money) and sterling M3 (broader money). These target ranges replaced the previous target ranges which applied to M1, sterling M3 and PSL2. It was further announced, and confirmed in the Budget for 1985/86, that in both cases, a steady reduction in the growth rate was envisaged over the next few years in order to reduce the inflation rate further over that period.

The adoption of M0, in preference to M2, as a target is due to two main reasons.

1. Unlike M2, the data on M0 can be traced back over a long period.
2. The belief of the authorities that M0 and M2 will, in any case, behave in a similar fashion; the bulk of M0 is accounted for by notes and coins in circulation, which are undisputed transaction balances and are therefore likely to behave in a similar fashion to other types of transaction balances.

From February 1984 the definitions of sterling M3 and M3 were slightly altered: the public sector sterling and currency deposits are now **excluded** from the definitions of sterling M3 and M3. This exclusion of the public sector sterling and currency deposits is because such deposits are both small and unlikely to influence economic behaviour.

RECENT EXAMINATION QUESTIONS

The following six questions taken from past papers give an indication of the type of questions you may encounter on 'Money'. You could usefully spend ten minutes or so on each question, trying to identify the main points you would use in your answers, before turning to the section on 'Outline Answers' which follow.

Question 1.

(a) What effect does inflation have upon money's ability to perform its functions?
(b) In what ways does the existence of money facilitate the workings of an economy?

Question 2.

(a) What is meant by the statement that money is the measuring rod of value? With what precision can changes in the value of money itself be measured?
(b) How well has money performed its function as a store of value in the United Kingdom for the past few years?

Question 3.

(a) What attributes must an asset possess in order to be considered liquid?
(b) To what extent do the following possess the attributes referred to in (a) necessary for them to be considered liquid:
 (i) Treasury bills;
 (ii) gilt-edged stock;
 (iii) banknotes;
 (iv) building society term shares;
 (v) certificates of deposit issued by a commercial bank?
(c) Classify the assets set out in (b) above according to whether they are included in the measures of the money stock in the UK.

Question 4.

Compare and contrast the principal liabilities of commercial banks and building societies with particular reference to the following:
(a) money as a medium of exchange;
(b) money as a store of value;
(c) the control of money supply.

Question 5.

(a) Distinguish between 'narrow' and 'broad' measures of a country's money stock.

(b) With reference to any country with which you are familiar, discuss the problems of defining 'narrow' and 'broad' money.

Question 6.

Some of the functions of money are performed by other liquid assets. What are these assets? Why are they held in preference to bank notes and bank deposits in the performance of these functions?

OUTLINE ANSWERS

Answer 1.

(a) Inflation may cause a loss of confidence in money's ability to perform its functions.

- Functions are affected to different degrees at various levels of inflation; therefore the rate of inflation is crucial.
- With the inflation rate up to about 2 ½ per cent p.a. (creeping inflation), money fulfils all its functions.
- As the rate of inflation increases, the 'store of value' is the first function to suffer: no one wants to hold on to a wasting asset. Non-monetary assets (antiques, old master paintings) begin to be preferred over financial assets. Savers demand a rate of interest at least equal to the rate of inflation.
- With further increases in inflation rate, the next function to suffer is the 'standard for deferred payments': upward adjustment clauses are built into future contracts (e.g. rent agreements) to avoid debtors gaining at the expense of creditors.
- The 'unit of account function' is next to suffer: adjustment to business accounts (inflation accounting) are needed.
- Finally, and rarely, if the inflation rate reaches astronomical levels (hyper-inflation), the 'medium of exchange' function suffers: people begin to revert to barter.

(b) Money generalizes purchasing power, and therefore:

- Makes possible division of labour and specialization; division of labour presupposes exchange: money helps in the payment of rent, wages, profit and interest; as a store of value and a standard of deferred payments, money enables investment of capital in plant, machinery, etc.; it streamlines the activities of banking and financial institutions as financial intermediaries, safely linking lenders to borrowers; it makes possible a higher standard of living in advanced money economies, via its four functions; it has a dynamic role as well: governments use monetary policies to achieve economic aims.

Answer 2.

(a) Brief explanation of the measure of value or unit of account function: by comparing prices of goods and services, it is easy to compare their values.

- *Brief* comparison of money and barter systems of exchange.
- Explain briefly the techniques, weaknesses and uses of various price indices.
- The value of money cannot be measured with exact precision.

(b)
- The rate of inflation rose sharply during 1979/80, progressively fell below 5 per cent in 1984, but rose to 5.9 per cent by September 1985.
- Money has not performed its store of value function effectively: wealth kept in cash and non-interest bearing accounts has fallen in value.
- With interest-bearing deposits and investments, money has better performed its store of value function: relatively high interest rates during the period, sometimes higher than inflation rate, creating real capital gain.
- Index-linking of financial assets protects the value of savings, but index-linked assets, being long-term investments, are not included in any measure of money, therefore irrelevant to a question about 'money'.

Answer 3.

(a) Attributes of liquidity:
- Quickly convertible into means of payments; such conversion without risk of monetary loss.

(b) (i) Treasury bills – quickly convertible into means of payments (i.e. through secondary markets), but suffer from risk of loss: their value during their 91-day life fluctuates in line with interest rate movements.

(ii) Gilt-edged stock – maturities vary, from five to 15 years to undated, but all marketable. Significant risk of loss in value because of their long maturities and high responsiveness to interest rate movements. Those close to maturity may be regarded as liquid.

(iii) Banknotes – most liquid: instant purchasing power without any risk of monetary loss. Inflationary loss irrelevant to this concept of liquidity because it relates to an asset maintaining its value in money, not 'real' terms.

(iv) Building society term shares – illiquid (except those nearing maturity): cash tied up for the term, or available on demand with significant penalty.

(v) Certificates of deposit – generally regarded as liquid: generally issued for short maturities (maturities may range from three months to one year); generally easily marketable in secondary money markets, therefore risk of loss due to interest rate charges is similar to that of Treasury bills.

(c)
- Treasury bills included in both PSL1 and PSL2.
- Gilt-edged stock not included in any measure of money or liquidity.
- Bank notes included in all measures of money.

- Building society term shares: those with less than 12 months to maturity included in PSL2, others not included in any measure of money or liquidity.
- Certificates of deposits included in sterling M3, therefore in M3. Those held by overseas residents are excluded from any measure of money or liquidity.

Answer 4.

(a)
- Only bank current accounts (not cheques) may be classed as medium of exchange: available as a *direct* means of payment.
- The cheques received by depositors from a building society may be used as a direct means of payment but these cheques are drawn upon a *bank current* account of the building society. Recent changes in money transmission services may blur the distinction between bank current accounts and building society ordinary accounts.
- All other bank and building society accounts do not act as medium of exchange: they have to be converted into cash or chequeable current accounts before performing the medium of exchange role – it is the *cash* which is withdrawn on demand that constitutes the medium of exchange, not the bank deposit from which it is withdrawn.

(b)
- Bank current accounts are not a store of value: they earn no interest.
- All other bank and building society accounts are a store of value: they all earn, albeit differing, rates of return; the term deposits generally earn the highest rate of return. If the reverse is the case, they provide a 'real' rate of pre-tax returns.
- Inflation rates higher than rates of returns tend to undermine their role as a store of value.
- Money in bank current accounts suffers from erosion in purchasing power during inflationary times.

(c)
- Define sterling M3 measure of the money supply.
- Traditionally the authorities have sought to control only bank deposits (together with notes and coins) in controlling the money supply.
- There is close substitutability between bank and building society deposits, hence the introduction of the wider liquidity aggregate PSL2.
- Define PSL2.

Answer 5.

(a)
- Narrow measures include assets which can be used instantly as a means of payment (give examples).
- Broad measures include narrow measure assets *plus* assets which may quickly and without significant loss be converted into the means of payment (give examples).

(b)
- Give full up-to-date definitions of M0 (narrow money).
- State why the M2 measurement was introduced (short-comings of M1), and why M0 was preferred to M2 as the narrow money target measure.

- Give up-to-date definitions of sterling M3 and M3 (with reasons for recent changes).
- Define the broad definitions of private sector liquidity: PSL1 and PSL2 (inclusion of liquid assets other than bank deposits because of substitutability among financial assets).
- Despite narrow and broad definitions – seven in all in the UK – there is still the problem of monitoring and controlling all potential purchasing power: unutilized credit facilities (overdrafts, credit cards, for example) are still not included in any aggregate.

Answer 6.

Briefly explain the concept of the liquidity spectrum, emphasizing the substitutability at the margins between real and near money assets.

- Near money assets perform the store of value function of money and, once removed, the means of exchange function.
- Near money assets held by the UK non-bank and bank sectors: postal orders, money orders, bills of exchange, building society deposits, National Savings securities and accounts, Treasury bills, local authority deposits, certificates of tax deposits, certificates of deposits, gilt-edged securities, money at call and short notice, and interest-bearing deposits with banks.
- Reasons for holding near money assets in preference to bank notes and current accounts with banks:
  (i)   Bank notes and current accounts with banks generally earn no interest, therefore inflation erodes their actual purchasing power – unattractive as a store of value.
  (ii) Near money assets provide a hedge against inflation, and sometimes a 'real' increase in the rate of return, therefore more attractive as a store of value.
  (iii) Most near money assets can be converted into cash or chequeable accounts fairly quickly and without significant loss of interest or capital, therefore larger payments can be planned easily and without financial loss in terms of near money assets.

A TUTOR'S ANSWER

The following question, in view of there being so many measures of money at present, is highly relevant. The answer highlights the fact that in a sophisticated modern economy there are many financial assets which perform some, if not all, the functions of money. Also that there is such substitutability among these assets in the public's mind that it is not possible to give one unambiguous definition of money as a whole in modern economies. The specimen answer should help you to assess the scope of the question, to make a relevant answer plan and to write within the scope of the question.

Question

Why is it difficult to provide an unambiguous definition of the money stock in a modern economy? Illustrate your answer by reference to any country with which you are familiar.

Answer plan:
(i) Money is easier to define in less developed economies.
(ii) In a modern economy there are many financial institutions and assets.
(iii) Money creates claims.
(iv) In the UK (country of reference), 'narrow' and 'broad' money.
(v) Official monetary and liquidity aggregates.

Specimen answer

It is relatively easy to define money in less developed economies because in these economies money is required to have intrinsic value (e.g. gold and silver) in order to be generally accepted as money. The developed economies, such as that of the UK, have devised numerous financial assets which are capable of performing some, if not all, of the traditional functions of money, namely, means of exchange, store of value, unit of account, standard of deferred payments. Money in the UK consists of claims, either on the government or on financial institutions.

In the UK a distinction is generally made between 'narrow' and 'broad' definitions of money, based on the concept of liquidity. Narrow money is simply defined as the most liquid assets, i.e. those possessing immediate purchasing power. Notes and coins in circulation with the public, together with bank sight deposits, could be said, by and large, to represent the sum total of immediate purchasing power in the UK economy. The problem, however, is whether there are other assets which are sufficiently liquid to be classed as money themselves. There is a dividing line, drawn by the concept of liquidity, between money and other financial assets. For an asset to be deemed liquid, it must be capable of being turned into 'cash' (notes and coins) or into a cheque account without 'significant penalty'. Significant penalty means: (a) loss or forfeit of a substantial amount of interest; or (b) a significant loss of capital value. According to this criterion, many assets are clearly not liquid. Thus, stocks (including government stocks) and shares may be sold quickly but their value can fluctuate considerably; houses can neither be sold quickly nor do they have a stable value; National Savings and some building society deposits cannot be cashed without significant penalties.

The narrow money definition emphasizes the means of exchange function of money. In the UK narrow money (notes and coins in circulation plus sight deposits of the public with banks) is a major component of M1, the narrow monetary aggregate. However, the monetary authorities (the Treasury and the Bank of England) have recognized certain deficiencies in M1 as an aggregate directed towards measuring the transaction balances – the immediate purchasing power – of the private sector. These deficiencies are:

1. The exclusion from M1 components of clearing banks' seven-day deposits which, although requiring notice of withdrawal, are in practice available on demand with very little penalty, and therefore are likely, in part at least, to be used as transaction balances.

2. The exclusion from M1 of building society deposits which (not term deposits) are widely used by the depositors in building societies as transaction balances.
3. The inclusion within M1 in recent years of a growing element of interest-bearing sight deposits, now over 25 per cent of the total M1. These volatile overnight deposits of large corporations and institutions are really investment funds rather than transaction balances.

Due to these deficiencies M1 became an ambiguous measure of narrow money. In order to rectify the situation, the authorities introduced in June 1982 a new monetary aggregate, M2, for defining narrow money in the UK. M2 includes all those assets which might legitimately be regarded as the transaction balances of the private sector, viz. notes and coins in circulation with the public, *plus* all non-interest bearing sight deposits, *plus* all deposits on which cheques may be drawn or from which standing orders, direct debit mandates or other payments to third parties may be made, *plus* other deposits of less than £100,000 having a maturity of less than one month. Thus for the first time National Savings Bank ordinary accounts and deposits of building societies within one year of maturity were included in the definition of narrow money in the UK. M2 is recognized by the authorities as an aggregate not so narrow as to be confined to cash and current accounts, but not so broad as to include investment balances (hence the exclusion from its components of deposits of £100,000 and over with more than one month to maturity), and as a monetary aggregate that sensibly comprises the 'transaction' balances of the private sector in modern times.

Despite this recognition of M2, the authorities unveiled yet another definition of narrow money, M0, in October 1983; in the Budget of 1984 it was M0, not M2, which was designated as the official narrow money target. The reason for this probably lies in the components of M0: it includes notes and coins in circulation with the public, *plus* till money of the banks, *plus* the banks' operational balances with the Bank of England. Whereas the data on M0 components are available for a long way back, the records on building society retail deposits and on National Savings Bank ordinary accounts – part of the M2 components – date only from March 1983. Also, the authorities believe that M0 and M2 will behave in a similar fashion, because the bulk of M0 is made up by notes and coins in circulation, which are undisputed transaction balances. These changes illustrate the problems confronted by the monetary authorities, both in defining narrow money unambiguously and in deriving data which can accurately measure the concept in question.

The need for broad definitions of money naturally developed from the narrow money definitions. Narrow money comprising immediately available purchasing power might well understate the *potential* purchasing power in the UK economy, given the existence of liquid assets with the private sector which could quickly and without significant loss be converted into immediate purchasing power. This led naturally to the development of broad money and liquidity aggregates. It is only a step further to argue that there are many other liquid assets which, as temporary abodes of purchasing power, are close substitutes for bank time deposits, and that these should be included to give a true aggregate of the immediate and potential liquidity held by the UK private sector. It was this thinking that led to the introduction of the PSL1 and PSL2 liquidity aggregates in 1979. PSL1 – the more restricted of the private sector liquidity measures – includes M1 *plus* private sector holdings of sterling time deposits with up to two years to maturity, together with other money market financial instruments (bank bills, Treasury bills, local authority deposits and certificates of deposit). PSL2 – a wider aggregate of private sector liquidity – consists of PSL1, *plus* private sector holdings of building society deposits (excluding term shares) and National Savings financial instruments (excluding National Savings certificates, SAYE contracts and other longer term deposits) *minus* building society holdings of bank deposits and money market instruments.

In addition to private sector liquidity aggregates, there is a wider monetary aggregate, sterling M3, introduced in the middle 1970s, which continues to occupy the centre of the stage as far as official targeting of broad money aggregates is concerned: in the Budget of 1984 it was established that M0 (as the narrow money aggregate) and sterling M3 (as the broad money aggregate) would be used as monetary target ranges for the financial year 1984/85. Sterling M3 consists of M1 *plus* private sector holdings of bank time deposits (maturity over two years) and sterling certificates of deposit.

In the UK, the private sector also holds foreign currency deposits with banks, which can be converted into cash and chequeing accounts, i.e. transaction balances. Therefore there has existed, since the early 1970s, a still broader monetary aggregate in the UK, namely M3. M3 consists of sterling M3 *plus* private sector holdings of foreign currency bank deposits.

In conclusion, it may be argued that there are two main reasons why it is difficult to provide an unambiguous definition of the money stock in a modern economy, such as that of the UK. First, in the developed economies the banking and financial institutions are sufficiently sophisticated to be able to create a growing variety of financial assets which are capable of performing some, if not all, of the traditional functions of money. Second, in the eyes of the public, there is substitutability, especially at the margins, among these financial assets.

A STEP FURTHER

If you wish to obtain up-to-date information on changes of definition of the various monetary and liquidity aggregates, then the *Quarterly Bulletin of the Bank of England* and the *Financial Times* are invaluable sources. There are also many useful articles on money which can be found in *Banking World* of The Institute of Bankers, and in the past editions of the *Financial Times*. These articles can be located by using the *Financial Times Monthly Index* in your college or public libraries. Fairly frequently you will find articles in the daily quality newspapers interpreting the definitional changes of monetary aggregates. Sometimes there are excellent programmes on the television dealing with various aspects of money. The Institute of Bankers publishes excellent *Updating Notes*, especially on definitional changes, and these keep candidates abreast of monetary matters.

Chapter 3   The UK financial system

- Appreciate the nature and functions of the United Kingdom financial system.
- Understand the nature of financial intermediation.
- Understand the structure, functions, operation and profitability of commercial banks through an analysis of the balance sheet.
- Distinguish between banking and non-banking financial intermediaries in respect of their liabilities, assets and functions.
- Understand the relationship of commercial banks to other types of banks and financial institutions.
- Revise the functions of the Bank of England as banker to the Government and banker to the banking system, including prudential controls.
- Understand the role of the Bank of England in the money markets particularly in relation to the techniques used for National Debt management.
- Distinguish between the retail and wholesale or complementary markets and understand the nature, functions and framework of a money market.
- Identify the participants in the London money markets and the monetary instruments used – the discount market, the sterling interbank market, the sterling and other currency certificates of deposit market, the eurocurrency market, the finance house market, the local authority market and the market for inter-company loans.

GETTING STARTED

To gain a clear insight into the mechanics of the UK financial system you need, first of all, to know the meaning of some collective terms used in connection with the financial markets.

The UK financial market itself is built around the functions of a number of 'financial institutions' and 'organized specialized financial markets' which operate within the UK economy.

The *financial institutions* may be classified into bank and non-bank financial intermediaries (BFIs and NBFIs). The BFIs constitute the UK *monetary sector*, which includes 'recognized' commercial banks, 'licensed' deposit-takers, the National Girobank, the trustee savings banks and the Banking Department of the Bank of England. Broadly speaking the money supply in the UK includes cash held by the public plus the deposits of the public with the monetary sector. The NBFIs are institutions such as the building societies, pension funds, insurance companies, unit and investment trusts.

The financial institutions are the repositories of the savings of the UK public and the main sources of funds to the UK public, and to each other. The major BFIs, viz. the clearing banks, differ from other financial institutions in that they provide efficient payment services to the nation.

The *organized specialized financial markets* match borrowers with lenders, whether for short-term lending in sterling (discount market, inter-bank market, certificates of deposit (CDs) market, finance house, local authority, commercial bill, and inter-company markets); for short-term lending in other currencies (dollar CDs and eurocurrency markets) or for long-term investments/loans (the Stock Exchange, including the gilt-edged security market). Each specialized market operates according to its own rules and regulations.

The financial institutions in the specialized financial markets of the UK financial system operate via 'financial instruments'. *Financial instruments* are methods of holding wealth by depositors and investors. *Bills* are short-term, fixed-yield securities; *bonds* are longer-term fixed-yield securities; *equity shares* have no fixed rate of return; *credits* in bank accounts, pass books and savings books reflect the amount of deposits, although interest rates vary. There is a wide variety of financial instruments, each with its particular features.

In the balance sheets of the financial institutions, savings received from depositors/lenders constitute the *liabilities* of these institutions, and loans and advances made to borrowers represent the *assets* of these institutions. Their liabilities, in the main, provide them with resources with which to create their assets.

Those among the BFIs and NBFIs which are *commercial*, *joint stock companies* have responsibility, like other financial institutions, not only for the safety of their depositors'/investors' money, but also for the profitability of their shareholders. This dual responsibility often creates a counter-pull – safety versus profitability – and the successful institutions have to resolve this dilemma.

The centre of the UK financial system is the *Bank of England*, the central bank of the UK. It supervises, monitors, guides and advises the financial institutions so that the government's monetary policy objectives are fulfilled in the interest of the nation.

ESSENTIAL PRINCIPLES

THE CENTRAL BANK

Most countries have a central bank as their principal banking institution, and as such it is under some degree of state control. It functions in close contact with the government department responsible for finance on the one hand, and with the country's financial institutions on the other, with the aim of meeting the needs of commerce, trade and industry.

The role of the central bank in the national economy relates to monetary control, supervision and financial assistance. Generally speaking, its main functions are as follows:

1. To implement the official monetary policy: basically this means varying the cost and availability of credit in the economy, thereby controlling money supply growth. It attempts to achieve this
   (a) by varying the terms of last resort assistance and other financial support, to relieve liquidity problems in the market;
   (b) by buying and selling government and other first-class bills in the money market;
   (c) by imposing direct controls on lending and interest rates;
   (d) by imposing restrictions on asset and liability management by the banks so as to control the 'credit multiplier' (see Ch. 4). The directives issued by the central bank to the financial institutions under its control are binding upon them.
2. To regulate the issue of the legal tender in order to meet the demand of the public for cash.
3. To act as the banker to the government,
   (a) by maintaining the accounts of the government departments;
   (b) by handling the government's short-term borrowing needs via the sale of Treasury bills;
   (c) by managing the issue, payment of interest, repayment at maturity or renewal of government stocks; i.e. managing the National Debt.
4. To act as banker to commercial banks by holding their transaction balances (e.g. for clearing in the UK), and assisting their settlement of mutual indebtedness and their payments to and from the public authorities.
5. To act as lender of last resort to the financial system, by lending to banks either directly or indirectly through open market operations.
6. To apply prudential control to ensure that financial institutions and markets are run soundly and honestly.
7. To stabilize the currency in foreign exchange markets, by intervening directly or through exchange controls.

Central banks are *not* responsible for implementing the fiscal policy of the government (i.e. management of the economy by varying the size and composition of taxation and public expenditure). They are *not* members of the International Monetary Fund; representation at the IMF is by member governments, although the central banks can act as its directors. They *are* members of the Bank for International Settlements (see Ch. 9).

FINANCIAL INTERMEDIATION

Whilst the inflow and outflow of funds provide the financial institutions with the major source of their profits, the process of channelling most of the savings in the economy to borrowers is also of great benefit to both the savers and borrowers and to the national economy. This process of matching the needs of the ultimate lenders with those of the ultimate borrowers, for a fee, is called *financial intermediation*, and the institutions performing the financial intermediation are known as the 'financial intermediaries' (FIs).

Financial intermediation has a number of important advantages over direct borrowing and lending; arguably these more than justify the cost of FIs, and also make the FIs indispensable to financially developed economies.

ADVANTAGES OF FINANCIAL INTERMEDIATION

Minimizing lending risks

Default

The main advantages of financial intermediation are as follows: Under direct lending, if the borrower fails to repay, then the lender may lose all or most of his capital. The risk of default is either removed or minimized if lending and borrowing take place via an FI. By interposing itself between the ultimate lender and ultimate borrower, the FI takes over from the lender the risk of loss through default by the borrower. The FI can do this for two main reasons.

1. By spreading its risks; through making a large number of loans of varying degrees of risks, returns and maturities, the FI can reduce its risk, and therefore the risks of the ultimate lenders. Besides, the FI can adjust its interest charges or fees to borrowers so that in the long run the loss through bad debts is covered.
2. FIs are traditionally financially sound institutions; their capital and reserves are sufficiently large and their deposit base is sufficiently stable to meet possible loan losses, whilst still protecting the funds of their depositors.

Loss of liquidity

Other things being equal, lenders prefer to lend short-term to avoid the loss of liquidity for long periods, especially if they suspect a possible need for liquidity arising, or an increase in interest rates occurring, before the borrower repays. On the other hand, borrowers prefer to borrow long-term to take full advantage of the productivity of the capital borrowed before it is to be repaid. The FIs are, by and large, able to resolve the problem of such opposing time-preferences by 'maturity transformation', i.e. borrowing short and lending long. Three main reasons enable the FIs to do this.

1. Unlike individual lenders or borrowers, FIs, due to their large-scale operations, are able to benefit from the statistical 'laws' of large numbers; e.g. the probability of an event occurring

comes closer to the probability of its not occurring, as the scale of operations gets larger. For example, the larger the number of accounts a bank holds, the greater the statistical probability that withdrawals will match, rather than exceed, deposits.

2. Their long experience enables FIs to anticipate seasonal changes in the outflow of their funds. They can therefore arrange to hold such interest-bearing assets as will mature in time to meet the seasonal pressure of outflow of funds.

3. By paying competitive deposit rates and by maintaining the confidence of depositors, FIs are able to maintain the overall level of their deposits while still providing their depositors with the benefit of liquidity: depositors are able to convert deposits into cash quickly and without loss of capital value.

Minimizing borrowing risks

Funds may not be available when required

Borrowers may be unable to obtain funds when needed, due in part to a shortage of funds from regular sources, and in part to a lack of knowledge of other sources from which funds may be available. The FIs are able to minimize this borrowing risk for two main reasons.

1. By aggregating the small savings of a large number of individuals, they are able to supply funds at the time borrowers *need* funds.

2. Unlike individual lenders and borrowers, FIs specialize in taking deposits from, and making loans to, many sources; hence they possess up-to-date information on the sources and terms under which funds are supplied and demanded.

Lenders may terminate lending at a time most inconvenient to borrowers

The FIs are able to minimize this borrowing risk via the fact that the economic basis of their financial intermediation lies in specialized large-scale operations. This enables them to:

1. spread default and other risks; and

2. hold a more balanced mix of asset portfolios, with regard to types and maturities, thereby reducing the risk of losses. FIs are therefore able to lend, on a contractual basis, such period loans as are most suitable to the needs of borrowers.

Borrowers wish to borrow at the lowest cost

First, due to their large-scale operations, FIs benefit from specialization and other economies of scale; hence they are able to keep their transaction costs down. Second, because the FIs are able to reduce lending risks, lenders are prepared to accept a lower rate of return from FIs. FIs are therefore able to lend at the lowest rates possible to borrowers.

The nature and practice of financial intermediation show that FIs are not just parasitic middlemen. Despite carrying liabilities (claims against them) which are more liquid than their assets (claims against borrowers), FIs are able to provide a unique financial service at minimum cost, assisting both ultimate lenders and borrowers *and*, via encouraging additional savings and investment, promoting economic growth for the nation as a whole.

BFIs AND NBFIs AS FINANCIAL INTERMEDIARIES

BFIs and NBFIs have some common fundamental characteristics: both rely on large-scale operations in order to benefit from statistical probabilities and from the economies which result from specialization in:

(a) matching anticipated changes in their liabilities and assets;
(b) remaining solvent despite their liabilities being more liquid than their assets.

However, there are some economists who argue that BFIs and NBFIs are very different kinds of FIs. Briefly they put their point of view as follows: when a BFI makes a loan, it creates a deposit of equal value (see Ch. 4). Therefore, the liabilities (deposits) of BFIs may be used actually to increase the volume of spending in the economy, because bank deposits are generally accepted in settlement of debts. In contrast, NBFIs merely *transmit* funds created elsewhere, i.e. notes and coins by the monetary authorities and bank deposits by the banking system. Hence BFIs, because they can create credit and thereby actually increase money supply, are different in kind from NBFIs who cannot do either of the two things. In one way this assertion is correct, in others it is not so.

It is true that, unlike BFIs, NBFIs cannot create credit via the 'credit multiplier', but they can add to the volume of spending in the economy, by enabling their borrowers to spend in excess of their current income. Suppose the NBFIs, by offering a better rate of return to savers than the BFIs, cause the BFI interest-bearing deposit holders to transfer some of their BFI time-deposits to NBFIs demand deposits kept with the BFIs; then, although the *total* of BFI deposits has not changed, their *composition* has altered: they now have less savings deposits and more demand deposits. The NBFIs can now make loans by drawing on their demand deposits, thereby increasing the volume of credit in the economy.

USEFUL APPLIED MATERIALS

CATEGORIES OF DEPOSIT-TAKING INSTITUTIONS IN THE UK

The 1979 Banking Act was passed with twin objectives: to protect depositors' funds, and to bring UK banking legislation into line with the EEC directive on the coordination of banking law in the Community.

With regard to the protection of depositors' funds, prior to the 1979 Act, there were many deposit-taking institutions in the UK financial system, which were effectively unsupervised, and the public perception of the different kinds of deposit-takers was extremely blurred. Under the Act, the Bank of England categorizes financial institutions into 'recognized banks' and 'licensed deposit-takers'.

To obtain the elevated status of a *recognized bank*, a financial institution must satisfy the Bank that it provides a wide range of banking services (e.g. the clearing banks), or a highly specialized financial service (e.g. discount houses), and that it fulfils minimum financial criteria and enjoys a high reputation and standing in the financial community. The financial institutions which enjoy the dignified status of a recognized bank are the clearing banks, the discount houses, the accepting houses, major British and overseas banks, and some finance houses and unit and investment trusts.

To qualify as a *licensed deposit-taker* (LDT), a financial institution must satisfy the Bank that it conducts its business in a prudent manner and that it fulfils certain minimum financial criteria appropriate to its level of operations.

The 1979 Banking Act has increased greatly the number of institutions subject to the supervision of the Bank of England. The Bank has the power to grant or withdraw recognition, to issue a licence or to amend a licence to 'recognized' status, subject in all cases to appeal to the Chancellor of the Exchequer. Any institution which is not 'recognized' or 'licensed' or 'exempt' from the Act is forbidden by law to take deposits or to carry on any banking business based upon the holding of such deposits. No new deposit-taking institutions can be established without authorization from the Bank of England.

The 'exempt' institutions are excluded from the arrangements under the Act because they are already satisfactorily regulated and supervised under separate legislation. The *exempted* institutions are building societies, the National Savings Bank, the National Girobank, the Banking Department of the Bank of England, insurance companies and pension funds.

THE UK MONETARY SECTOR

Since 1981, the monetary authorities have established a much wider UK monetary sector. The Bank of England recognizes the following institutions as the participants of the new, widened monetary sector: recognized banks, LDTs, the trustee savings banks, the National Girobank, the Banking Department of the Bank of England and some banks in the Channel Islands and the Isle of Man. It is noteworthy that not all major financial institutions are included even in the widened monetary sector. The notable exceptions are building societies, the National Savings Bank, insurance companies and pension funds.

The institutions in the UK monetary sector most relevant to the Monetary Economics examination are the commercial banks, the Bank of England and the discount houses. A detailed knowledge of the functions of these institutions is therefore essential for candidates taking the Monetary Economics examination.

THE COMMERCIAL BANKS

As commercial enterprises, these aim to make profit for their shareholders, to whom they are accountable. The main UK commercial banks are the London Clearing Banks (Barclays, Lloyds, Midland, National Westminster and Coutts), the Scottish Clearing Banks (Bank of Scotland, Royal Bank of Scotland, Clydesdale Bank), the Northern Irish Banks (Northern Bank, Ulster Bank, Allied Irish

Banks, Bank of Ireland) and someother joint stock banks, who are not, like the London clearing banks, members of the Bankers' Clearing House, and whose cheques and credits are cleared via members of the Clearing House (Isle of Man Bank, C. Hoare and Co., Yorkshire Bank).

Sometimes the clearing banks, especially the London clearers, are called 'retail' banks on account of their vast branch network serving the banking needs of hundreds of thousands of personal and corporate customers. However, the distinction between 'retail' and 'wholesale' banks – e.g. the merchant banks, who provide for the specialized financial needs of large corporate customers and therefore do not require the expensive branch network – has blurred in recent years. Most clearers are now 'banking groups', providing through their subsidiaries retail *and* wholesale banking and non-banking services 'under one roof'. They have acquired controlling interests in merchant banks and finance houses, and they have opened leasing and factoring companies and have set up unit trusts. They have established offices overseas for foreign operations and have a substantial share in the eurocurrency market, both directly and in conjunction with the London-based consortium banks. Their main role, however, is to act as financial intermediaries for the sterling and currency funds.

The clearing banks may be distinguished from other banks by the extent to which they provide current account facilities and money transmission services; because of this distinction, the volume of their demand deposits forms a major component of the total purchasing power in the UK economy. It is also for this reason that they are sometimes called 'primary' banks, as distinct from 'secondary' banks which (with the exception of some American and Japanese banks) take term deposits and not sight deposits. Therefore secondary banks, unlike primary banks, cannot provide money transmission services. The *secondary* banks include accepting houses, merchant banks, foreign banks, consortium banks and unit and investment trusts.

THE BALANCE SHEET APPROACH

The best way to determine the structure, functions and operations of commercial banks, say clearing banks, is by analysing the items on the liabilities and assets sides of their balance sheets.

The liabilities side

Capital and reserves

These represent amounts owed to the bank's equity (and preference) shareholders. The bank must show profit in its operations in order to pay adequate dividends to its shareholders. Profitability is therefore very important to a commercial bank.

Loan Capital

These are the aggregate fixed-interest commitments of the bank; loan interest must be paid before any dividend distribution to shareholders.

Customers' sterling deposits

The volume of these deposits forms the largest liability of a bank, but it is also the main source of its profitable operations; banks pivot the credit multiplier on the deposits they take, which generally comprise the following:

1. *Current account balances.* These are safe repositories of immediate liquidity; banks operate their money transmission services through these accounts. Either no or modest interest is paid to current account holders; but the holders of large overnight balances, usually big corporate customers, receive interest on call accounts, which are similar to current accounts.
2. *Seven-day deposits.* These are an excellent example of 'near' money assets, yielding a rate of return yet convertible into cash or current account on demand, with only a seven-day interest loss in lieu of notice.
3. *Term deposits.* These cannot be withdrawn by depositors before the end of the term; long-term deposits are 'wholesale' deposits and tend to be larger in amount than 'retail' deposits which are generally small sight and other easily withdrawable deposits.

Customers' currency deposits	At present there are no exchange controls in the UK and therefore UK residents, personal and corporate, can hold deposits in foreign currencies of their choice. These currency resources assist banks to participate in the eurocurrency markets. Banks pivot the *currency* credit multiplier on currency deposits as they do the ordinary credit multiplier on their sterling deposits. Note that if a bank fails, then its sterling and currency depositors are treated as a special class of creditor with increased rights and are paid before its loan stock holders or any class of shareholders. This shows that the safety of depositors' funds is of paramount concern to the banks.
Certificates of deposit	These are really large receipted term-deposits with one major difference, that the receipts are bearer documents which are therefore easily marketable and negotiable items in the CDs market. Since they are liquid-cum-safe investments, banks selling them offer a lower interest rate than on term-deposits.
Other liabilities	These include amounts owing at the balance sheet date, such as the proposed dividend to shareholders, amounts due to subsidiary companies in the 'group' and to the Inland Revenue towards corporation tax commitments.

The assets side

The assets of a bank result from the deployment of its loan and share capital and its deposits. The following are the main assets of a commercial bank.

Liquid assets	These are immediately available:

1. To meet cash withdrawals from demand deposits, e.g. notes and coins in the till.
2. To effect clearing settlements and to meet unforeseen contingencies – e.g. non-interest bearing operational balances with the Bank of England (not including the ½ per cent of eligible liabilities); these balances are treated as cash.

Money at call and short notice	Includes funds lent to discount houses to help them balance their books (outflow of funds on bills discounted and on purchases of Treasury bills and other short-term financial assets *minus* the inflow of funds from the

maturity of discounted bills and from the sale of other short-term financial assets); also funds lent to stockjobbers and stockbrokers, to money and bullion brokers, to corporate customers and to other banks (the latter can be very important). Money 'at call' means that it is repayable by the borrower on demand. Money 'at short notice' implies that a notice of repayment of up to 14 days will be given by the lending bank. These monies are usually secured loans (always so in the case of discount houses) and earn interest; the rate depends upon the availability of such funds and the period of loan. After cash, these are the most liquid assets of a bank. These funds provide a suitable outlet for the surplus liquidity of the banks, and are therefore the principal means by which banks adjust their cash and liquidity requirements.

Cheques in course of collection	These represent claims of the bank for items to be collected to its credit from other banks in the payment mechanism.
Eligible bills	The Bank of England is prepared to buy these first class, easily marketable bills, mainly from discount houses. Items qualifying as eligible bills are Treasury bills, local authority bills and first class trade bills which have been accepted by eligible banks. Banks do not usually tender for Treasury bills directly but buy them from discount houses later on, as part of their easily realizable short-term assets. Local authorities also issue bills to raise short-term funds. The holding of eligible bills forms a significant percentage of the total assets of a bank. They are held because they provide a safe rate of return and are easily discounted by the discount houses in the bill market in the course of open market operations.
Certificates of deposit (CDs) and other market loans	Although a bank's holdings of CDs issued by other banks represents its short-term investments, these can easily be cashed at current rates in the CDs market. The market loans are short-term loans made to non-bank borrowers via specialized markets, to other banks via the inter-bank market and to other large customers; these loans are, of course, linked to the London Inter-Bank Offered Rate (LIBOR).
Investment other than trade investments	These are safe short- and medium-term fixed interest rate investments, mainly in gilt-edged securities of the central government. Besides being quite safe, these instruments are held both for their yield, and also for the possibility of capital gain, which occurs when interest rates fall. However, even though they are liquid, there is the danger of financial loss on realization if the current market interest rates are higher than those operating when the asset was purchased.
Advances and loans to customers	These items form the largest proportion of a bank's assets and are traditionally seen as the most profitable. They include all types of bank lending to personal and corporate customers. In theory, overdrafts, but not fixed-term loans, are call money, but in practice, very rarely would a bank call for their immediate repayment. In fact, therefore, these balances represent a bank's illiquid assets, as they are assets which are prone to lending risks; this point is reflected in the higher interest rates banks charge on them. A bank widely diversifies

its advances and loans in terms of maturity and sectors. Changes in these balances have a significant influence upon the size of the money supply. Short-term loans, e.g. an overnight loan to I.C.I., are very liquid; whereas loans that have a definite repayment period have a liquidity that is determined by the time to maturity.

Investment in subsidiary and associate companies	A subsidiary is a company in which the bank has controlling power; an associate company is one in which it owns at least 20 per cent of the share capital. Most commercial banks, especially the clearers, are now fully-fledged banking groups providing banking and non-banking services 'under one roof'. Their investments in *subsidiary* companies assist them in providing services beyond the range of traditional banking services, such as factoring, leasing, insurance, estate agency. Their investments in *associated* companies often provide the commercial banks with the means through which to operate their banking services more efficiently, e.g. Bankers' Automated Clearing Services.
Trade investments	Investments in a company in which the investor has a less than 20 per cent stake are called trade investments; these investments give a bank access to specialist services, as with the Agricultural Mortgage Corporation, Finance for Industry and the Bankers' Clearing House. Trade investments may also assist it in opening overseas offices, e.g. in conjunction with a consortium bank.
Non-operational balances with the Bank of England	The Bank of England requires all institutions in the monetary sector with 'eligible liabilities' (broadly speaking, its sterling deposit liabilities, excluding those with an original maturity of over two years, and any sterling resources obtained by switching foreign currencies into sterling) of £10 million or over, to:

1. Keep ½ per cent of its eligible liabilities in non-interest bearing and non-operational balances with the Bank. This cash-deposit ratio is designed to provide the Bank with a major source of its income for market operations. These may take place in order to relieve a shortage (or surplus) of cash in the money markets, or to influence short-term interest rates.
2. Be ready to receive 'calls' for special deposits from the Bank. As a part of the UK monetary control regulations, the Bank of England is empowered to call, from time to time, for non-operational but interest-bearing special deposits from the institutions in the 'monetary sector' (see Ch. 4) with eligible liabilities of £10 million or more. Such calls for special deposits are a means of withdrawing cash from the money market, thereby reducing the commercial banks' credit multiplier because of their frozen funds in special deposits.

Premises and equipment	These are a bank's fixed assets, which are necessary for its operations. They include head office and branch bank premises, other buildings, computers, equipment and vehicles. The book value of a bank's premises and other buildings represents hidden reserves.

The asset structure of a bank reflects a successful compromise between its two main, but conflicting, objectives: safety of its depositors' funds and profitability for its shareholders. If the composition of a bank's liabilities changes, e.g. more current accounts and less saving deposits, then its asset structure will be adjusted accordingly, with more liquid assets and less long-term investments.

The move to composite rate tax deductions on banks as well as building society deposits has led to much more competitive pricing of deposit rates by the banks.

FOREIGN BANKS

In 1960 there were only 77 foreign banks in London; however, by the end of 1982, their number was around 450. They are represented in London through branches, subsidiaries, representative offices and through minority holdings in 'consortium banks', i.e. institutions which specialize in international banking activity and which are owned jointly by a group of established banks.

Foreign banks are attracted to London for several reasons:

1. To participate in the eurocurrency transactions, because London is a major eurocurrency market (see Ch. 9).
2. To serve the financial needs of companies from their own countries which are operating in the UK.
3. To participte in financing trade between the UK and their own countries, and indeed between the UK and other countries.
4. To have stakes in consortium banks.
5. To cater for specific ethnic communities now resident in the UK.

Therefore, the presence of foreign banks is not restricted to London; some banks are establishing networks of strategically- placed offices in major UK cities, for example, in Birmingham, Bradford and Liverpool.

The regulatory changes of the past few years, viz. capital adequacy ratios and liquidity criteria, have not in fact driven off any foreign banks. Instead their role as LDTs and recognized banks under the 1979 Banking Act has continued to develop successfully in the UK. Cumulatively, the foreign banks now account for over 60 per cent of total UK bank assets and 27 per cent of lending to UK customers (16 per cent of all sterling advances and 72 per cent of foreign currency advances).

Among the foreign banks, the American and Japanese banks are the most prevalent. Therefore, for statistical purposes, the Bank of England classifies foreign banks as American Banks, Japanese Banks and Other Overseas Banks. In terms of balance-sheet trading, the American banks account for around 45 per cent of foreign banks' business in London, and around 12.5 per cent of all lending to British corporate customers. Their prowess in oil and energy finance has enabled them to take a sizeable slice of the North Sea oil business. Probably the most aggressive banks currently operating in London are the Japanese. Their share of UK lending has more than doubled since 1977.

The American and Japanese banks, along with a few other foreign banks, are engaged in UK domestic wholesale banking, and in particular, in providing funds to large companies. They are also competing with the UK clearing banks in retail banking in sterling, particularly that denominated in foreign currencies. In August 1985 the total of the UK private sector sterling and foreign currency deposits with the American and Japanese banks was £4634 million and £5871 million respectively. Their sterling and foreign currency advances to the UK private sector on the same date amounted to £7974 million and £15,862 million respectively. Together the American and Japanese banks account for well over 40 per cent of total foreign currency deposits with all banks in the UK.

THE BANK OF ENGLAND

It is the central bank of the UK and as such its relationship with the Treasury and its functions and operations in the UK financial system are of extreme importance.

Adviser and agent to the UK government

One of its main (perhaps *the* main) functions is to act as the adviser and agent to the UK government in formulating and implementing the official monetary policy. It is uniquely placed, on account of its specialized knowledge, contacts and experience of the UK financial market acquired over many years, to give advice to the government on the technical aspects of monetary policy as it is being formulated. Its advisory role has widened in recent years: the Bank officials serve on a wide range of official committees concerned with economic and monetary matters, bringing to these committees the Bank's economic forecasts and views on financial matters. Thus the monetary policy, when finalized, is likely both to be in line with government objectives and to meet with a large measure of agreement from within the financial community.

Since the Bank is the agent of the government for implementing monetary policy measures, its 'advice' to banks and to other financial institutions has to be obeyed. In implementing monetary policy, the Bank seeks to influence both the cost and availability of credit; this can be done by varying the terms of 'last resort' assistance to the banking system, by making calls for special deposits, by introducing direct controls on bank lending and interest rates, and by reactivating the Minimum Lending Rate, i.e. its lending rate to the money markets (see Ch. 5).

Banker to the government

It is the banker to the government, and in that capacity its activities include:

1. Maintaining the accounts of government departments.
2. Arranging for the government's short-term borrowing needs by handling the weekly issue of Treasury bills.
3. Acting as registrar to the gilt-edged stock holders, thereby providing for the long-term borrowing requirements of the public sector, paying interest, arranging renewal or redemption at maturity and issuing new gilt-edged stocks. In effect, the Bank acts as the manager of the National Debt.

4. It holds and protects the UK gold reserves and manages the UK foreign currency reserves via the Exchange Equalization Account (EEA). It often uses its management of the EEA to stabilize the foreign exchange value of the pound sterling against other currencies in the foreign exchange markets.

5. As the bankers' bank, it holds their operational balances, their current accounts, which the banks use for obtaining cash and for settling clearing and other transactions among themselves and with the public sector.

6. As the central note-issuing authority in the UK, it is responsible for the printing, issue, withdrawal and destruction of bank notes. Whilst the note issue is free of interest, the interest-bearing securities acquired by the Bank in using some of the note issue results in profit to the Bank; this profit is credited to the Treasury accounts.

7. A traditional role of any central bank is as lender of last resort, whereby it makes funds available when the banking system is short of liquidity. The Bank of England, in performing this traditional function, uses a unique method: it does not relieve shortages in the UK banking system (which may be due to large net payments to the Exchequer on account of tax payments or to sales of gilt-edged securities) by lending *directly* to the banks; rather it does so *indirectly*, by buying eligible bills, invariably from the discount houses, at prices acceptable to it. The discount houses can then return the call and short-notice money to the banking system, thereby removing the banks' liquidity shortage; the discount houses can also continue to cover the weekly Treasury bill issue (see below).

8. The Banking Act 1979 makes the supervision of the monetary sector a function of the Bank of England; it supervises recognized banks and LDTs to ensure that they are soundly run, so that any recurrence of the 1974 banking crises can be avoided, although individual banks, e.g. Johnson Matthey do sometimes get into trouble. More generally, the Bank has responsibility for overseeing the soundness of the UK financial system as a whole.

THE DISCOUNT MARKET

The main participants of this market are the twelve discount houses which are members of the London Discount Market Association. Discount houses are specialized institutions; they borrow mainly from the banking system and invest by discounting commercial bills and purchasing short-term assets, chiefly Treasury bills and gilt-edged securities. The discount houses constitute a buffer between the Bank of England and the banking system and it is through them that the Bank, as lender of last resort, regulates the availability of its funds to the commercial banks, thereby relieving shortages of liquid funds within the banking system.

It is very important that the mechanics of *how* the Bank of England performs its traditional role of lender of last resort are clearly understood. The present arrangement of relieving cash shortages of the banking system involves the Bank purchasing bills exclusively from the discount houses; the latter maintain a portfolio of eligible bills, purchased with the funds deposited with them, according to the eligibility requirements of the eligible banks.

The clearing banks inform the Bank of England daily of the target level of daily balances they are aiming at. On the basis of this, and the Bank's own estimate of flows between the banks and the public sector, the Bank assesses the size of the likely shortage (or surplus) of its balances each day. The shortage (or surplus) is announced on the morning of each day to the money markets. The Bank then informs the discount houses that it is prepared to buy bills from them, or to sell bills to them. The discount houses then offer bills to the Bank at prices of their own choosing. The Bank may or may not accept the prices offered, but will always relieve the shortage, or surplus, at a price acceptable to itself.

Until 1981, the Bank of England could have lent to the discount houses directly at the *Minimum Lending Rate* (MLR). In 1981, MLR was suspended (in January 1985 it was reactivated for one day) and direct lending by the Bank to the discount houses is now used much less frequently. Instead, bill purchases, primarily commercial bills within the four bands of various maturities (see below), have become the pivot of the system by which the Bank provides its lender of last resort assistance to the banking system, through the discount 'window'.

The Bank has defined a number of 'maturity bands' which refer to the periods remaining before the bills mature. Band One has bills from one to 14 days to maturity; Band Two, 15 to 33 days; Band Three, 34 to 63 days; and Band Four, 64 to 91 days. While the Bank mainly concentrates on dealing in bills within Bands 1 and 2, dealings in Bands 3 and 4 are not uncommon. As well as outright purchases of bills, the Bank sometimes engages in sale and repurchase agreements with the discount houses, i.e. the Bank provides funds to the discount houses by buying bills from them with an arrangement that the discount houses will buy the bills back on an agreed day.

The discount market is one means by which commercial banks can adjust their liquidity positions, because the discount houses mainly borrow surplus funds from the banks on a call/overnight basis. Thus the discount market provides a highly suitable and profitable place where the banks can place their surplus-to-need liquidity on a call basis.

The discount market is an important provider of short-term finance to business companies; it does this by discounting commercial bills of exchange. In fact, the discount houses are market makers in commercial bills, and to promote the bill market the Bank of England took two interrelated steps: first, it increased the number of eligible banks and second, as a condition of eligibility, obliged them to hold a minimum of 2½ per cent, and an average of 5 per cent, of their sterling deposits in secured loans with discount houses. This ensured that discount houses had sufficient funds at their disposal for their bill operations.

The discount houses compete in underwriting the weekly Treasury bill tender. They maintain a secondary market in certificates of deposit, and are prominent in the short-dated gilt-edged securities market.

The discount market is the oldest money market for short-term funds and is often referred to as the 'traditional' money market. The newer money markets which have emerged since the 1960s, and in particular the inter-bank and certificates of deposit markets, are known as 'parallel' or 'secondary' money markets.

In the balance sheet of a discount house, the largest item, by a long margin, in its sterling and currency liabilities relates to funds it has borrowed from the banking sector. And the largest item on its assets side, again by a long margin, is 'other bills', i.e. bills other than UK and Northern Ireland Treasury bills. These statistics reflect the complementary relationship between the discount houses and the commercial banks and the importance of commercial bills in the discount market.

Instruments used in the money markets

These are markets in which wholesale funds (large sums) are lent and borrowed for relatively short periods. The most important markets within the money market are the discount market, the inter-bank market and the certificates of deposit market.

The instruments used in the bill market include 'bills', which are short-term securities issued by borrowers (government – Treasury bills, companies – commercial bills, local authorities – local authority bills) to obtain short-term finance. The lenders (bill holders) keep the bills as 'near' money assets.

Treasury bills are issued by the Bank of England on behalf of the government in amounts ranging from £5000 to £1 million (the minimum tender is £50,000), usually for a period of 91 days. There is no interest on Treasury bills and therefore these are issued below par and repaid at par; the capital gain is in lieu of interest rate. The discount houses agree to cover the entire weekly issue; the sale proceeds provide the short-term funds needed by the central government.

Commercial bills become eligible bills when accepted by an eligible bank – mainly the UK commercial banks and the larger overseas banks. 'Accepting' literally means guaranteeing for a fee that the bill will be paid at maturity. Bills of exchange accepted by banks are called 'bank bills' and are easily marketable before maturity at the 'finest' rates, i.e. the person selling or discounting a bank bill receives a higher price for it.

Local authority bills are 'receipts' issued by the borrowing local authority needing funds in advance of its yearly rates inflow. To obtain large sums quickly, from seven days to a year, the local authorities operate through bill brokers and merchant banks. These bills are quickly marketable. Discount houses play an important part in making local authority bills liquid.

SECONDARY STERLING MONEY MARKETS

The certificates of deposit (CDs) market

CDs are receipts issued by banks certifying that a deposit has been made of a certain sum, for a given period, and at a particular rate of interest. The depositor or the holder will be paid in due course by the issuing bank at maturity of the CD. Sterling CDs are issued by London banks, in multiples of £10,000, with a minimum of £50,000 and a maximum of £500,000, for periods ranging between three months and five years. On CDs issued for a period of less than one year, interest is paid at maturity, along with the capital sum invested. For CDs issued for periods longer than one year, interest is payable annually. CDs are flexible instruments which offer advantages to both the depositor and the borrower. The depositor obtains for his minimum £50,000 investment maximum security, a good rate of interest and easy marketability in the secondary CDs market at current rates. For the original borrowing bank, a CD is a fixed period loan, and therefore not withdrawable until the expiry of that period.

Sterling inter-bank market

This is a short-term wholesale market where banks lend to each other for periods from overnight to five years. The minimum amount of loans is £250,000, normally unsecured. The rates of interest in this market for overnight money are higher than those offered in the discount market for call money. The inter-bank rates are known as LIBOR. The fundamental significance of the inter-bank market to the UK banking system is not only that it, together with the CDs market, is the largest sterling parallel market, but also that it, like the discount market, allows individual banks to adjust their liquidity positions quickly. Banks with surpluses can lend on the inter-bank market to banks with shortages, thus reducing the need for individual banks to keep large holdings of liquid assets; this increases their profitable lending operations.

The development of the market for CDs and the inter-bank market in the early 1970s has had an important effect on how the UK banking system works. Before these markets existed, whilst a bank could increase its deposits by offering higher interest rates, it could not be sure of doing this by a given amount quickly and with certainty. Thus, prior to the existence of these markets, a bank's lending activity, and therefore profitability, was to some extent limited by the amount of its customers' *retail* deposits. Nowadays, however, banks have much more flexibility. Banks with surpluses can lend wholesale funds in the inter-bank market to other banks with shortages, while banks with shortages can also borrow large sums by issuing CDs. Recently the clearing banks have had to raise large deposits from the inter-bank market. This reflects the success the building societies have had in garnering retail deposits, and then recirculating them back to the banking system, at higher rates, through the inter-bank market.

The finance house market

The major finance houses have been 'recognized' by the Bank of England as 'banks', but there are many other finance houses which still operate to meet the needs of the consumer demand by offering hire purchase facilities for consumer durables. Due to the tight monetary policies during the past two decades, including a credit squeeze applying to instalment buying facilities, a major proportion of finance houses' funds has been channelled to meet the needs of business companies, mainly through their two main services:

1. *Factoring*, i.e. taking over the debtors of a company – sometimes up to 80 per cent of the invoice value – in return for cash. This arrangement has helped business companies considerably in coping with their cash flow problems, especially during the economic recession of the past decade.

2. *Leasing,* this is an alternative to hire purchase or long-term borrowing as far as the business companies are concerned. The finance house buys expensive capital goods, including ships, aircraft, and machinery, for company clients, and leases the item to the client on agreed regular lease payments during the life of the item. Leasing helps companies to obtain capital goods they require in times of low profits and credit shortage. Some finance houses have joined 'credit clubs' to provide the unsatisfied financial needs of property developers and medium-sized business firms; this has encouraged the banking side of their business and has made them competitors to banks.

As NBFIs, the proportion of capital and reserves to borrowed funds differs widely in the balance sheets of individual finance houses. However, their liabilities side shows that the main sources of their funds are loans and deposits from the banking sector, discounted bills and deposits from business companies and individuals. Since finance houses are considered by the public as being less secure than banks and building societies, they have to offer higher rates to attract funds from corporate and personal sectors. The major asset item in their balance sheets is the provision of funds for hire purchase transactions, mainly for cars, to households and firms. It is a comparatively small secondary market.

The inter-company market

The severe qualitative and quantitative restrictions placed by the authorities on bank lending in the late 1960s meant that the banking sector was unable fully to meet the financial requirements of the business companies. The finance houses to some extent bridged this gap. The development of inter-company markets was a device to get around official credit restrictions: e.g. company A, needing funds, drew a bill of exchange on company B with surplus funds; company B accepted the bill and obtained a higher rate of interest from company A, and company A got it discounted in the bill market and obtained funds; thus both the lending and borrowing companies benefited from the arrangement. The market has continued, but in a limited way, even after the relaxation of the tight credit restrictions.

The finance house market and the inter-company market are rather limited extensions of the inter-bank market, each providing the participants with opportunities to adjust their liquidity positions.

The sterling 'parallel' or 'secondary' markets in London comprise, chronologically, local authority, finance house, inter-bank, inter-company, and certificates of deposit. In connection with these markets as a whole, two points are of significance.

1. They do not work in isolation from each other; lenders and borrowers are interwoven.
2. They are largely uncontrolled markets; therefore any direct official control on lending and interest rates which is not uniformly applied to all financial institutions triggers off disintermediation and 'round tripping'. This upsets the validity of the sterling M3 statistics and loosens the hold of any official restrictions imposed via monetary policy.

RECENT EXAMINATION QUESTIONS	The following six recent questions have been asked in the Monetary Economics papers of the Banking Diploma of The Institute of Bankers. These questions reflect the type and depth of knowledge required to answer questions placed in the UK Financial Sector section of the syllabus. First try to locate, from the contents of this chapter, the main points you consider essential in answering each of these questions. Then spend ten minutes or so planning your answer to each question before turning to the section on 'Outline Answers' which follows.
Question 1.	What is meant by the term 'financial intermediary'? To what extent are banks the principal financial intermediaries?
Question 2.	Assess the role of the so-called 'parallel' sterling London money markets in the present-day UK financial system.
Question 3.	Outline the present functions of the London discount market. To what extent has the role of discount market within the financial system changed since 1970?
Question 4.	For what reasons does a commercial bank need liquidity and how may it be provided? How has Bank of England supervision in this area evolved since 1981?
Question 5.	With particular reference to the Bank of England's day-to-day operations in the money markets, discuss the Bank's present role as 'lender of last resort'. How has this role changed since 1981?
Question 6.	(a) Using the figures given in Table 1 as a guide, assess the role of the UK banks in channelling finance for trade and industry. (b) What other figures are needed in order to prepare a complete assessment of the adequacy of bank finance for trade and industry?

Table 1   UK Banking Sector (Sterling)

	Deposits from UK residents	Lending to UK residents (including holdings of securities issued by public and private sectors)
	(£m.)	(£m.)
Public sector:		
Central government	518	6,128
Local authorities	241	4,881
Public corporations	383	600
Private sector:		
Industrial and commercial companies	11,133	24,169
Personal sector	24,901	11,259
Other financial institutions	5,357	3,534
	42,533	50,571

Note: The discrepancy between the two columns is due to the omission of non-deposit liabilities, such as capital and reserves, and to the omission of data relating to overseas residents.

OUTLINE ANSWERS

Answer 1.

Financial intermediary – an institution which links an ultimate lender with an ultimate borrower: banks link depositing and borrowing customers; building societies link depositors and mortgagors; pension funds and insurance companies link contributors and policy holders with the companies in which they invest their capital. They are the 'go-betweens', linking surplus economic sectors with the deficit sectors, and deficit and surplus units within the same sector.

Banks are arguably the principal intermediaries, because:

- the liabilities of central and commercial banks only are accepted as money in the official monetary definitions;
- other financial institutions maintain accounts;
- banks' balance sheet totals (including eurocurrency deposits) are extremely large.
- NBFIs (building societies, insurance companies, superannuation funds, unit and investment trusts) may be considered principal financial intermediaries, but at the longer end of the time scale.
- it is when ultimate borrowers and lenders by-pass banks, not other financial institutions, that disintermediation results.

Answer 2.

- Parallel sterling London money markets are specialized short-term money markets. Discount market and eurocurrency market are *not* included.
- Chronological order: local authority deposits, finance house deposits; inter-bank; inter-company and CDs.

- In order of size: inter-bank first; inter-company last.
- These markets provide:
  (i) liquid assets for participants – banks (including clearers and accepting houses), local authorities and companies (companies are able to buy and sell CDs);
  (ii) profitable lending opportunities for participants;
  (iii) LIBOR (London Inter-Bank Offered Rate) plays a significant role in the inter-bank market in:
  (a) determining the cost of market-related borrowing by the banks' customers,
  (b) calculating the internal cost of funds charged to banks' branches by their head office, and
  (c) determining the level of base rates.
- Parallel money markets play no direct role in the Bank of England's implementation of monetary policy.

Answer 3.

Present functions of discount market (mainly the 12 discount houses):
(i) to act as a buffer between the Bank of England and the commercial banks;
(ii) to be one means by which commercial banks can adjust their liquidity positions; discount houses borrow surplus funds of the banks on a call/overnight basis;
(iii) to be an important provider of short-term finance to companies via discounting commercial bills (commercial bills far outweigh Treasury bills); discount houses are market makers in commercial bills;
(iv) to continue to underwrite the weekly Treasury bill tender;
(v) to maintain the secondary market in CDs, and to be prominent in the short-dated gilt-edged securities market.

Changed role of the discount market within the financial system:
- Despite many changes of detail, the market remains the vital buffer between the commercial banks and the Bank of England; the liquidity of the banking system is still regulated by the Bank dealing with the discount houses as 'lender of last resort', rather than by dealing directly with the banks.
- Competition and credit control enforced the buffer role of the market by including 'money at call and short notice' as part of the banks' reserve asset ratio; this money enabled, and enables, discount houses to underwrite the weekly tender of Treasury bills.
- 1981 changes in monetary control techniques: monetary authorities
  (i) have preferred to purchase bills from the market rather than engage in direct lending;
  (ii) have required the 'eligible banks' to maintain a minimum of 2½ per cent (and an average of 5 per cent) of their deposits in secured loans with the market to provide it with adequate funds to maintain the market in bills;
  (iii) have determined that the Bank of England's assistance to the financial system via bill transactions is to be exclusively with the discount houses.
- The growth of the inter-bank market during the 1970s has provided an alternative to discount houses for individual banks

wishing to adjust their liquidity – this has reduced the profits of discount houses, hence the 1981 requirement on eligible banks.

Answer 4.	<ul><li>A bank needs liquidity: (i) to meet cash withdrawals from deposits; (ii) to effect clearing settlements via operational balances with the Bank of England; (iii) to meet unforeseeable problems in financing known future commitments; (iv) to maintain the confidence of the public.</li><li>It provides for liquidity by maintaining a certain percentage of its assets in liquid assets (e.g. Treasury bills, call money with discount houses, short-dated gilt-edged securities).</li><li>Factors relevant to liquidity considerations: (i) the extent of diversification in its deposit base; (ii) its ability to raise deposits when needed from the inter-bank market and the CD market; (iii) the cash flow generated from maturing assets.</li><li>Liquidity criteria applicable to all banks: the Bank of England ensures that individual banks are adopting prudential policies in the light of their individual circumstances, taking into account all the factors relevant to liquidity.</li></ul>

Answer 5.

- Bank of England's traditional role as lender of last resort: it makes available funds when the banking system is short of liquid resources.
- In its day-to-day operations in the money markets, the Bank carries out this role involving eligible bill purchases only from the discount houses.
- The eligible banks have to maintain an average of 5 per cent, and a minimum of 2½ per cent of their eligible liabilities in secured money with discount houses; these funds the discount houses use in their bill dealings.
- The Bank announces a daily estimated shortage (or surplus) of 'cash'; it is prepared to buy eligible bills from discount houses which are offered at *their* own prices, but which the Bank may not accept. The Bank will however make good any shortage at a price acceptable to it. With the sale proceeds, discount houses discount more bills.
- The shortages often arise in the banking system, given large net payments to the government for sales of gilt-edged securities, tax payments, etc.
- Main changes since 1981: virtually no direct lending to discount houses; abandoning the weekly announcement of the MLR, to which direct lending was generally linked (MLR was reintroduced for one day in January 1985); bill purchasing within four bands, depending upon maturity of the bill, is now the pivot of the 'lender of last resort' role; main change in carrying out this role is in the method of operation; discount houses remain the buffer between the Bank and the commercial banks.

Answer 6.

(a) The scope of the question: how the banking system functions in transforming deposits into loans, and how these loans finance trade and industry.

- Given figures show that the main source of the banking sector's sterling deposits are from the personal sector and that the majority of bank advances are to trade and industry rather than to private individuals.
- Banks mediate between one sector of the economy and another, and at the same time cause 'maturity transformation': the majority of balances lent are demand deposit balances and loans and advances are generally not repayable on demand.
- Funds provided by banks take the form of overdrafts (the classic British way of bank finance), loans of various types and maturity (these are becoming increasingly important), discounting of bills and the purchase of stocks and shares (finance to the Government and industry).

(b) Additional information needed on following points for a complete assessment of the adequacy of bank finance for trade and industry: how much do trade and industry rely on other sources of finance (e.g. new issues, loan stock, trade credit, government grants and loans); is there a large unsatisfied demand for funds (short- medium- long-terms) from trade and industry? Are trade and industry being crowded out of the available bank finance by the demands of the public sector?

A TUTOR'S ANSWER

The following question touches on various important aspects of the UK financial system and its institutions. The tutor's answer is intended to help you establish the scope of the question and then to write cohesive, relevant information in answering the whole question.

Question

Describe the present role and assess the significance of the following in the UK banking system:
(a) the discount market,
(b) the inter-bank market.

Specimen answer

The question requires up-to-date knowledge of the present roles of the discount market and the inter-bank market, and the significance of each market to the UK banking system.

The London discount market consists of 12 discount houses and a few small firms of bill brokers. The market is an integral part of the UK financial system. It is basically concerned with borrowing and investing short-term money. The main activities of the discount houses are:

1. To make a market in bills and other short-dated financial instruments.
2. To provide a remunerative outlet for other banks' liquid funds, but to hold these deposits as short-term liabilities available on demand to the depositing banks.
3. To cover in full the weekly Treasury bill tender which is an essential part of the government's short-term borrowing arrangements.
4. To provide short-term finance to the private sector by discounting bills of exchange.

5. To play an active role in the secondary market for the sterling and dollar certificates of deposit by providing ready marketability for the CDs.
6. To provide the Bank of England with a medium through which it can influence movements in short-term interest rates.

The central point of significance of the market within the UK banking system is that it provides the Bank of England with a reliable channel through which the Bank controls the liquidity of the banking system as a whole.

In 1981, three important changes took place in the Bank's money market operations:

1. It began to rely less on direct lending to the discount houses and to favour buying bills from them to offset 'cash' shortages and surpluses in the banking system.
2. It stopped the practice of telling the discount houses the prices at which it would buy bills; those houses who now wish to sell bills to the Bank have to formulate their own prices, and the Bank decides which prices to accept.
3. The Bank ceased the practice of creating shortages in the money market by the deliberate over-issue of Treasury bills and then relieving the shortage at its own terms.

These changes gave increased importance to the Bank's open market operations in bills. To promote the bill markets, the Bank took two related steps:

(a) it increased the number of 'eligible' banks whose acceptances it was willing to buy;
(b) it ensured that the discount market, the main market-maker in bills, had sufficient funds at its disposal: the Bank obliged the 'eligible' banks to hold a minimum of 2½ per cent and an average of 5 per cent of deposits in secured and interest-bearing loans to the discount houses and bill brokers. The rate at which the Bank buys and sells commercial bills is an important indicator of the Bank's desired level of short-term interest rates, and of the marginal cost of funds to banks.

The fundamental role of the inter-bank market, like the discount market, lies in providing a mechanism whereby banks can adjust their liquidity. It is predominantly a market in short-term unsecured loans between banks. The main bank lenders of the funds in the market are merchant banks, overseas and foreign banks in London, savings banks, the clearing banks and their subsidiaries and the non-bank lenders (e.g. pension funds, commercial and industrial companies, insurance companies). The amounts involved range up to several million pounds and, although funds can be placed from overnight to a period of years, the market is essentially short-term. The main interest rate which prevails in this, the largest of the sterling parallel markets, is the London Inter-Bank Offered Rate (LIBOR).

The fundamental significance of the inter-bank market to the UK banking system is not only that it (together with the CDs market) is the largest sterling parallel market, but also that, like the discount market, it is a key market which allows individual banks to adjust their liquidity positions; banks with surplus funds lending to those with shortages. The existence of this highly developed market tends to reduce the need for individual banks to have large holdings of liquid assets, because short-falls in cash flows can now be met by borrowing on the inter-bank market. The Bank of England, however, does not stand as lender of last resort to the inter-bank market and therefore the market cannot relieve shortages of 'cash' when all banks are short of liquidity. It is then that the open market operations of the Bank of England became still more significant.

LIBOR is of extreme importance to the banks; many commercial loans are directly linked to LIBOR, and bank base rates are set with reference to inter-bank rates. This is because inter-bank rates determine the marginal cost of a bank's funds. The levels of LIBOR and other inter-bank rates are influenced by the level of short-term rates desired by the Bank of England.

A STEP FURTHER

This section of the Monetary Economics syllabus requires a lot of study. What you learn in this chapter impinges on other parts of the syllabus. However, changes in the UK financial system do not occur frequently. Therefore, once the current system is clearly and fully grasped, and your knowledge is kept up-dated, you should be able to answer regularly-asked questions on this topic in the Monetary Economics question paper, which invariably seek precise information.

To keep abreast with changes as they occur, you need to up-date your knowledge by reading *Banking World*, Bank of England *Quarterly Bulletin*, The Institute of Bankers *Updating Notes* and *Examiners' Reports* and the financial press.

A comprehensive knowledge of the UK financial system is essential to your understanding of other topic areas within Monetary Economics.

The Banking Information Service have published a very useful book, *A Guide to the British Financial System*, which covers the fundamentals of the UK Financial System.

Chapter 4

Money supply

Understand and interpret the causes and effects of changes in the money supply.

- Revise the process of credit creation and the constraints on the growth of bank deposits.
- Understand the concept of money base control.
- Identify the key factors which cause the money supply to increase and, in particular, analyse the effect of the following on the money supply figures:
  (a) The Public Sector Borrowing Requirement,
  (b) Public sector debt sales to the bank and non-bank sectors,
  (c) Bank lending to the private and public sector,
  (d) Borrowing in foreign currency,
  (e) The Balance of Payments.
- Be able to identify distortions in the money supply aggregates from factors such as inflation, high interest rates, exchange rate changes, arbitrage, trends in mortgage lending, etc.
- Appreciate the interrelationship of changes in the money supply and changes in the bank balance sheet.
- Understand the techniques used for control of the money supply. Briefly outline UK monetary policy, post-1971.

GETTING STARTED

In Chapter 2 we saw how difficult it was to give one all-embracing definition of money, and we considered the reasons for such difficulty. We also noted that in most money-using economies, money supply, or money stock, has two types of definition: the narrow and the broad definition.

Under the *narrow* definition, the money supply of a country is comprised solely of the means of payment, i.e. the total money available to the public for spending. This money is made up of the notes and coins (the cash) in *circulation* and the demand deposits held by the public in financial institutions: it is often referred to as 'spending' money. The distribution between cash and demand deposits depends entirely on public preference and the degree to which the financial system has developed. When a demand deposit holder cashes a cheque at his bank, the amount of deposits held by the bank is reduced and the amount of cash in circulation with the public is increased. The cash in *tills of the banks* is excluded from spending money because it is not directly available to the non-bank public for spending.

The *broad* definition of money supply comprises not only the spending money at the disposal of the non-bank public, but also 'near' money assets, because these can be converted with little difficulty and financial penalty into spending money. For money supply control purposes, monetary authorities may use either narrow or broad money definitions or some combination of both.

The quantity of money in a country is determined both by the actions of the non-bank public (consumers and businesses), and by the decisions and actions of the commercial banks, central bank and the government.

ESSENTIAL PRINCIPLES	Demand deposits with commercial banks form a major part of the real or spending money in a country with a developed banking system.

ESSENTIAL PRINCIPLES

MONEY-CREATION BY COMMERCIAL BANKS

Demand deposits with commercial banks form a major part of the real or spending money in a country with a developed banking system. Cash, which forms a very small part of the total spending money, is provided by the central bank. If the commercial banks could increase the volume of demand deposits, without causing a reduction in the amount of cash in circulation, they would therefore increase the quantity of spending money in the country.

The banks are in fact able to do this, for two main reasons.

1. Demand deposit holders have full confidence in the ability of banks to pay cash on demand. Therefore the public accepts payments by cheques, and other means provided by banks, because it is both more convenient and safer than receiving payments in cash.
2. Whenever a bank makes a loan to a customer, somewhere in the banking system a deposit of equal value is created. When the banks are increasing the supply of loans (their assets), their deposits (their liabilities) are also increasing by an equal amount.

Suppose there is only one bank in a community, and the public, with absolute confidence, deposit their surplus cash in that bank. Customer A deposits £100 cash, which is surplus to his immediate spending needs, with the bank, which credits A's account. The bank's liabilities (A's deposit) and assets (£100 in the till) have increased by the same amount. Let us assume that the bank, as a matter of policy, keeps 10 per cent of all deposits in cash or near cash assets to meet customers' withdrawals of cash. The bank can on-lend £90 from A's

£100 deposit to, say, customer B. The bank then credits B's current account and debits B's loan account with £90; once again banks liabilities and assets have increased by the same amount. Most probably, B has borrowed £90 to repay a debt for purchasing goods or services, say, from C. C accepts B's cheque for £90 with confidence, and deposits it in his account at the bank. The liabilities and assets are not affected by this transaction, because the credit of £90 is now in C's account and the debt of £90 is still in B's loan account. The bank is now able to advance £81 (£90 less 10 per cent liquidity cushion) to, say, customer D.

The process of receiving deposits, on-lending them (less 10 per cent) and creating more deposits can continue until the total amount of deposits, or spending money, created by the bank on the basis of A's £100 cash deposit reaches £1000; i.e. the bank has increased the narrow money supply by a multiplier of 10.

The *credit-creation multiplier* measures the amount of new deposits created from the original deposit. It can be measured by the following formula:

$$\frac{\text{Total value of new deposits created}}{\text{The value of original deposit}}$$

The fact that in real life there are several banks does not invalidate the credit-creation principle. Although the assets and liabilities of the *individual banks* connected with the process of the above £1000 credit-creation may increase by larger or smaller amounts, the liabilities and assets of the *banking system as a whole* will increase by £1000.

When in response to a greater demand for cash by the public the central bank issues, via commercial banks, an additional supply of cash, most of the additional cash will 'seep' into bank deposits, enabling banks to start the credit-creation process. For example, a bank may increase its deposits by buying securities from an individual or firm or by buying government securities; in each case the bank increases the deposits of the vendors *and* its own liabilities by the same amount. Note that banks' liabilities, in the shape of deposits, constitute money.

CAN BANKS CREATE MONEY INDEFINITELY?	The above example might give the impression that banks, if they chose, could create money indefinitely. This is not the case. There are certain factors which constrain the banks' ability to create money indefinitely.
Cash leakages *Internal*	Suppose, in the above example, B needs some cash, and therefore deposits, not £90, but £80. This will reduce the banks's ability to create credit.
External	If there are no foreign exchange restrictions, then bank customers can transfer funds overseas, perhaps to earn a higher rate of return. Such transfers of funds overseas reduce the credit-creation multiplier.

Customer demand for loans	If the economy has been suffering a long period of recession, then the level of business profits will be low and the level of unemployment high. Consequently, the demand for loans by the private and personal sectors would be low. Banks are seriously hampered in credit-creation if the non-bank public *do not want to borrow*. The banks could lower interest rates charged to borrowers and attempt to attract demand for loans. Other things being equal, a decrease in interest rates extends the demand for loans by the non-bank public, especially by business firms, because lower borrowing costs increase their profitability. Conversely, an increase in interest rates contracts demand for loans by firms and households; they will defer such purchases as can be deferred until borrowing costs come down.
Self-imposed constraints	Banks will not knowingly risk their depositors' funds or their own surplus resources if there is a likelihood that the loan they give may become a bad debt. Banks may not lend, especially in times of economic recession, to firms which are on the verge of bankruptcy. Therefore credit-creation may not take place to the extent that the demand for loans at the prevailing interest-rate would allow.
Liquidity cushion	To maintain the confidence of the non-bank public in the banks' ability to cash cheques on demand, and to avoid a 'run' on themselves, prudent banks keep a cash-reserve-to-deposit ratio in cash and near-cash assets. The higher this liquidity ratio, the smaller the credit-creation multiplier. In addition to a self-applied prudential liquidity ratio, the central bank may impose on the commercial banks' liquidity its own prudential requirements, e.g. they may be obliged to maintain a specific reserve-to-deposit ratio in liquid or near-liquid form. Such official constraints on the banks' liquidity would curb their ability to create credit.
Government policy	Money supply in developed economies is ultimately under the control of the monetary authorities. If the authorities fear that the banks are exceeding the desirable level of credit-creation, they may in the interest of the national economy ask the central bank to restrict the ability of the commercial banks to lend. This may be done by asking for some form of deposit at the central bank that will reduce the commercial banks' ability, and indeed desire, to lend, or it may be done by direct instruction.
PROFITABILITY VERSUS SAFETY	Commercial banks are business organizations. They market financial services to make a profit, from which to meet their running and capital costs and to distribute dividends to their shareholders. Like most other commercial enterprises, they usually aim to maximize profits. In theory, maximizing profits requires that they should on-lend all the deposits they take at the highest rate possible; this might mean lending to the riskiest borrower for the longest period of

time! However, in practice, banks cannot neglect the safety of their deposits. Sound banking demands a fine balance, which *both* maximizes safety for their depositors' funds and maximizes dividends for their shareholders. Banks solve the dilemma of safety versus profitability by maintaining a prudent liquidity cushion in the form of cash in tills, operational balances with the central bank, loans to money market on a call or short notice basis, first-class commercial bills, government short-dated bills and certificates of deposit issued by other banks. After the liquidity cushion portfolio is satisfactorily constructed, banks make advances. Making advances is traditionally a bank's major activity and the interest on them is its main source of profit. Banks may also buy long-term, fixed-interest government securities, partly for security and partly because they produce a higher income than near-money assets.

MONETARY BASE CONTROL (MBC)

The non-bank public cannot get an additional supply of immediately spendable money except by drawing it from their deposits with the commercial banks. The commercial banks, in turn, cannot get an additional supply of such money except by drawing it from their operational balances with the central bank. Therefore, technically, the main source of additional, immediately spendable money supply, i.e. cash, for banks and non-banks is the operational balances of the commercial banks with the central bank. 'Monetary base' or money base is the name for the banks' operational balances with the central bank. The clearing banks maintain base money with the central bank to make payments among themselves, between themselves and the government and to obtain cash for their customers.

The theory underlying the MBC method is that the central bank, by regulating the growth of base money, can control the growth of money supply directly. Suppose that the commercial banks maintain a *consistent* ratio between their deposits and the base money, either voluntarily or because the central bank requires them to do so. The central bank, by announcing that the base money would grow by a specific percentage over specific periods, would then be able to regulate the growth in base money and, indirectly, in bank lending, in line with the official money supply growth rate target. Note that the key to the success of MBC is that the assets of the monetary base on which the credit-creation multiplier is pivoted must be *completely* in the control of the central bank.

There are a few problems, however, associated with the MBC method.

1. Since the time deposits cannot be withdrawn before maturity, there is little need to maintain a specific and constant ratio between the amount of time deposits and base money. Banks could sidestep MBC simply by increasing the *proportion* of time deposits, and thereby increase lending. To avoid this happening, the central bank could require commercial banks to maintain a prescribed ratio between base money and *all* deposits.

2. There is nothing to stop banks from maintaining base money in *excess* of the prescribed requirement. They would then have flexibility to increase lending, and to create credit, whenever it was most profitable to do so; for instance, when the demand for loans was very high, so that higher interest rate could be charged to borrowers. Unfortunately this might be the very time when money supply would already be increasing! In order to stop money supply overshooting its growth targets, the central bank might have to push up interest rates to very high levels. Wide fluctuations in interest rates would create uncertainty, and adversely affect the national economy. In any case 'distress borrowing' is interest inelastic.

Some economists suggest that if the MBC method is to be used to control the money supply growth, then 'wide' base money should be the basis for control. *Wide base* money includes the operational balances of commercial banks with the central bank, *plus* notes and coins in circulation and in bank tills (in the UK this is M0).

USEFUL APPLIED MATERIALS

MONEY SUPPLY IN THE UK

In the March 1984 Budget, the Chancellor of the Exchequer set target ranges for 1984/85 money supply growth in terms of M0 and sterling M3. Similar targets were set in March 1985 for 1985/86. These targets replaced the previous targets which had applied to M1, sterling M3 and PSL2 (see Ch. 2). Thus the current measure of *narrow* money supply is M0, and of *broad* money is sterling M3. However, for the control of *overall* money supply growth, the sterling M3 aggregate is used by the monetary authorities. The main reason why the authorities have considered sterling M3 to be, since 1976, the most important money supply aggregate, is that there is a well understood relationship between sterling M3 and changes in the banks' holding of assets.

COUNTERPARTS OF STERLING M3

These can be understood more easily by reference to the items in the liabilities and assets sides of the balance sheet of the banking system.

Liabilities	Assets
Sterling deposits of UK residents	Sterling lending to UK private sector
Sterling deposits of overseas residents	Sterling lending to UK public sector
Foreign currency deposits	Sterling lending to UK overseas residents
Net non-deposit liabilities (capital and reserves *minus* land, buildings, etc.)	Foreign currency lending

The entries in the above balance sheet can be simplified as follows:

Net overseas sterling lending = Sterling lending to overseas residents *minus* sterling deposits of overseas residents.

Net foreign currency lending = Foreign currency lending *minus* foreign currency deposits.

Net currency and external lending = Net foreign currency lending *plus* net overseas sterling lending.

Since the total liabilities must equal total assets, the *increase* in total liabilities must equal the *increase* in total assets. Hence:

1. The increase in sterling bank deposits of UK residents must equal the increase in sterling bank lending to UK private sector, *plus* the increase in sterling bank lending to UK public sector, *plus* the increase in the banks' net currency and external lending, *minus* the increase in the banks' net non-deposit liabilities.
The Public Sector Borrowing Requirement (PSBR) is the amount by which public sector (central government, local authorities and public corporations) payments exceed public sector receipts. The PSBR can be financed by the monetary authorities in four ways:
   (a) by increasing cash in circulation;
   (b) by selling government debt to the UK non-bank public,
   (c) by borrowing foreign currency from overseas;
   (d) by borrowing from the banking sector.

Therefore:

2. The increase in sterling bank lending to the UK private sector must equal the PSBR,
minus the increase in cash held by the public,
minus the sale of government debt to the UK non-bank public;
minus public sector borrowing of foreign currency from overseas.
   When the government spends that part of the PSBR it has borrowed from the banks, private sector deposits with the banks will increase by the same amount.

Therefore:

3. The increase in sterling deposits of UK residents must equal the increase in bank lending to the UK private sector,
plus the PSBR,
minus the increase in cash held by the public,
minus sales of public sector debt to the UK non-bank public,
minus public sector borrowing of foreign currency from overseas,
plus the increase in the banks' net currency and external lending,
minus the increase in the banks' net non-deposit liabilities.
'Public sector borrowing of foreign currency from overseas' and 'the increase in the banks' net currency and external lending' are

normally put together under the heading of 'net external and currency flows'.

We can now see the clear relationship between sterling M3 and its counterparts.

4. The increase in sterling M3 must equal the increase in sterling lending to the UK private sector,
    plus the PSBR,
    minus the increase in cash held by the public,
    minus sales of public debt to the UK non-bank public,
    plus/minus net external currency flows,
    minus the increase in banks' net non-deposit liabilities.

The counterparts to sterling M3 are published with the money supply figures by the monetary authorities.

FACTORS WHICH CAUSE CHANGES IN THE MONEY SUPPLY

1. A very large proportion of money supply in the UK is made up of bank deposits. Therefore, anything which affects bank deposits affects money supply.
    The size of the PSBR and the sources from which it is financed significantly influence bank deposits and money supply aggregates:
    (a) if an increase in PSBR is financed by *borrowing from the banks* then, when the borrowed sum is spent by the public sector, it creates new bank deposits in the banking system, without any offsetting leakage; hence the money supply increases.
    (b) if an increase in PSBR is financed by *increasing the supply of cash*, e.g. the Bank of England printing more notes, then, to the extent that the public hold more cash, money supply will increase directly. The rest of the additional cash will increase bank deposits and that will, of course, also increase money supply.
    (c) if an increase in PSBR is financed by the *sale of government securities to the UK non-bank public*, then the money supply will not change because the payments by the non-bank public for their purchase of public debt will reduce money supply (bank deposits) by the same amount by which the public sector spending will increase it.
    (d) if an increase in PSBR is financed by *borrowings from overseas and in foreign currency*, this will not affect the sterling deposits of the banking sector and therefore money supply will not change.
    (e) If an increase in the PSBR is financed by the *sale of government securities to overseas residents*, then money supply will increase by the amount of their purchases.

2. The sterling lending by the banking sector to the domestic non-bank sector and to the overseas borrowers will, provided the overseas borrowers spent their borrowings in the UK,

considerably increase money supply. Since every loan creates a deposit somewhere in the banking system, all sterling lending by banks will increase money supply in its own right; at the same time it will also enable the banks to operate the credit-creation multiplier, which will increase money supply still further.

3. The official financing of the balance of payments deficit or surplus (see Ch. 7) will affect money supply figures. Financing a deficit broadly means that money is leaving the country; hence it is causing a reduction in money supply. Conversely, financing a surplus broadly implies that money is coming in which, when spent, will increase bank deposits and therefore money supply.

4. If the *building societies* and the branches of *foreign banks in the UK* offer better terms to depositors than those offered by the UK banks, and thereby attract deposits then this will, in the first instance, reduce the deposits of the UK banks. Since there are no exchange controls in the UK, some of the deposits *lost* by the UK banking sector may be invested overseas in search of better returns. This may cause a semi-permanent reduction in money supply until the interest rates offered in the UK become competitive with overseas rates.

5. The stance of the monetary policy (see Ch. 5) will have a bearing on the banks' capability to lend and to create deposits. If the monetary policy is contractionary, it may require banks to keep a cash-to-deposits ratio, and may also place qualitative and quantitative lending restraints on banks. All these policy requirements will reduce money supply, unless banks are able to get reserve funds from uncontrolled sources and are able to find ways of lending without transgressing the official requirements.

6. An increase in the banks' non-deposit liabilities will reduce their funds for lending and, therefore, reduce money supply. The net non-deposit liabilities of a bank equal the total of its capital and reserves *minus* its land, buildings, capital equipment and the like. However, a decrease in the net non-deposit liabilities of banks, to increase loans and investments, will not increase sterling M3, because they are not a component of sterling M3.

DISTORTIONS IN MONEY SUPPLY (STERLING M3)

There are factors which cause distortions in the sterling M3 money supply aggregate over which the authorities have little control. Such distortions reduce the reliability of sterling M3 as an indicator of monetary conditions in the UK.

1. One of the chief factors causing this kind of distortion is *disintermediation*. Disintermediation is a process which is triggered whenever the authorities place any direct quantitative controls on bank lending, and leads to a greater amount of lending business being routed through uncontrolled institutions and markets. It may also result in the market developing new instruments that are **not** covered by direct controls, by other restrictions or by the monetary aggregates.

In order to cope with direct controls, e.g. lending ceilings and reserve asset ratios, banks begin to lend and borrow from institutions and markets which are free from direct controls. This causes disintermediation, i.e. an unrecorded increase in money supply: although the money supply increases, the sterling M3 figure does not register the increase, since it takes place via uncontrolled channels and instruments.

2. When a quantitative control is suspended or removed, there is the *re-intermediation* effect on money supply, i.e. the unwinding of disintermediation. The lending business which was previously re-routed through uncontrolled channels *returns* to the banking system, causing an 'increase' in the sterling M3 aggregate, without actually increasing money supply or having much effect on monetary demand in the economy.

3. If banks succeed in taking away from building societies some of their mortgage loan business, then sterling M3 will 'grow' faster than it actually does; this is because building society lending, unlike bank lending, is not a component of sterling M3.

4. If the authorities increase taxes to reduce money supply or partly to finance the PSBR, bank customers may borrow from banks to pay the increased taxes; this will increase, and not decrease, money supply, at least in the first instance.

Overfunding and the 'bill mountain'. During 1984 and 1985, the UK authorities have deliberately sold more gilt-edged stocks and National Saving securities to the non-bank public than was necessary to finance the government's borrowing requirement. The reason for such overfunding was largely to counteract a very large increase in bank lending to UK residents. The authorities argue that they are seeking to control the money *supply* and not just loan demand.

This overfunding led to a reduction in sterling M3 and to persistent liquidity shortages in the money markets. The Bank of England has sought to relieve these shortages by purchasing commercial bills from the market on a very large scale. As a result of these very large-scale open-market operations, the Bank has become a major holder of commercial bills, in a sense, a direct lender to the private sector. Overfunding the PSBR in this way has resulted in the volume of commercial bills held by the Bank rising to over £11 billion – the so-called 'bill mountain' in October 1985.

An increasingly important development with regard to the size of PSBR, has been the sale of private sector assets (British Telecom, for instance). The revenue from these sales *reduces* public sector borrowing; it does not provide means for financing it.

RECENT EXAMINATION QUESTIONS

The following six questions should give you an idea of the types of questions that can be set on the 'Money Supply' section of the Monetary Economics syllabus. First try to identify from the text the main points you would use to answer these questions. Then spend ten minutes or so planning your answer to each question before turning to the section on 'Outline Answers' below.

Question 1.	For what reasons does a commercial bank need liquidity and how may it be provided?

Question 2.	Discuss in detail the main factors which cause changes in the money stock.

Question 3.	Explain in detail how an increase in government borrowing influences.
	(a) the money supply,
	(b) conditions in the money markets.

Question 4.	What effects do changes in a country's money stock have on its commercial banks?

Question 5.	Discuss the view that changes in bank lending, and *only* changes in bank lending, cause changes in sterling M3.

Question 6.	Discuss how far a country's money stock comprises:
	(a) liabilities of its central bank,
	(b) liabilities of its commercial banks.
	Does it usually comprise the liabilities of other financial institutions and if not, why not?

OUTLINE ANSWERS

Answer 1.

Knowledge of a new approach to measurement of banks' liquidity is essential (*Bank of England Quarterly Bulletin*, September 1982).

(a) A bank needs liquidity:
- to meet withdrawals of deposits by customers;
- to meet inter-bank clearing settlements (for this banks must keep operational balances with the Bank of England, in addition to a ½ per cent deposit);
- to meet unforeseeable problems in financing known future commitments;
- to provide for time differentials in cash flow arising from its deposits being repayable at shorter notice than its loans;
- to provide a cushion against bad debts;
- to maintain the confidence of the public.

(b) A prudent bank provides for liquidity by maintaining a *certain* percentage of its assets in:
- cash in till;
- operational balances with the Bank of England;
- money at call and short notice;
- Treasury bills and first-class bank bills;
- short-dated gilt-edged securities;
- CDs.

(c) The *certain* percentage of liquidity depends on

- the extent of diversification in its deposit base (demand and period deposits),
- the ability to raise funds from the inter-bank market;
- the cash flow generated from its own maturing assets.

Answer 2.

Explain the effects of changes in the counterparts to sterling M3:
(i) *increase in PSBR* increases money supply, unless funded by the sales of government securities to the non-bank public;
(ii) *increase in bank lending to the private sector* will increase money supply;
(iii) *a deficit in the balance of payments* broadly reduces money supply (money flowing out) and a surplus increases money supply (money flowing in).

Changes in interest rates, quantitative and qualitative controls and reserve ratios will influence bank lending, which will affect money supply.

Answer 3.

(a) If the government borrows from the:
   (i) banking system – money supply will increase;
   (ii) non-bank public and overseas in foreign currency – money supply will remain unchanged.

Changes in the counterparts of sterling M3 cause changes in sterling M3.
(b) If borrowing is from the:
   (i) banking system – liquidity will increase and put a downward pressure on very short-term interest rates;
   (ii) non-bank public – the liquidity effect is neutralized, and the operational balances of banks with the Bank of England are first reduced, and then increased by the same amount.

Beware the common fault: government borrowing does not *automatically* mean higher interest rates. An increase in PSBR means that sterling M3 goes up and, in the first instance at least, interest rates will fall.

Answer 4.

Bank deposits are a major part of the money stock.
- Increase in the money stock will increase bank deposits.
- Increased deposits enables increased lending; increase in profitability of retail banks (no change in interest rate is assumed).
- Profitability of wholesale banks will fall, as margins of bid and offered interest rates narrow.
- Increase in the money stock may lead to economic growth (if there is spare capacity) and a consequent increase in consumer spending.
- Increase in consumer spending and imports provides an opportunity for increased bank lending and services.
- If the increase in the money stock is excessive, then interest rates may fall and diminish retail banks' profits.

● If the money stock decreases, the above effects will be reversed.

Answer 5.

Bank deposits are a very large part of sterling M3.
● Counterparts of sterling M3.
● Sterling M3 is affected by changes in bank lending, but there are *other* counterparts of sterling M3.
● Other factors: balance of payments, interest rates, non-deposit liabilities of banks, currency borrowing from overseas, monetary policy.
● Disintermediation and re-intermediation.
● Wrong to say that *only* changes in bank lending cause changes in sterling M3.

Answer 6.

● Definition of the money stock – M0 and sterling M3.
● Definitions showing money performing *some* functions and *all* functions.
● Liabilities of the Bank of England (UK's central bank) – notes held by the public, not coins.
● Liabilities of the commercial banks – sight deposits; time deposits.
● Ratio of central bank liabilities and commercial bank liabilities to the total money stock are about 20 : 80 in the UK (60 : 40 in developing countries).
● Liabilities of other financial institutions, e.g. savings banks, building societies, are included in Public Sector Liquidity, but not in the money stock because their deposits do not fulfil *all* the functions of money – they are near money.

A TUTOR'S ANSWER

The following question deals with various aspects of money supply. The specimen answer is intended to help you establish the scope of the question, so that you write relevant information when faced with similar questions in an examination.

Question

Define the measure of money supply in the United Kingdom known as sterling M3. Explain how sterling M3 would be directly affected by each of the following:
1. an increase in sales of gilt-edged securities by the Bank of England;
2. the payment by companies of value-added tax;
3. an increase in sterling bank lending to the overseas sector.

Answer plan

● Briefly define sterling M3 and state its latest components.
  (a) Who purchases? Only the direct effects of purchases asked.
  (b) Are current accounts of companies reduced?
  (c) Are there matched increases in lending and deposits?
● Explain only the direct effects; avoid second-round effects.
● Keep asking: does a direct effect cause changes in the *components* of sterling M3?
● Once the effects are technically and correctly explained, *stop*.

Sterling M3 is the official monetary aggregate in the UK which measures the 'broad' money in the country. It comprises 'real' money (immediate purchasing power) *plus* 'near' money (real money, once removed).

The Bank of England definition of the sterling M3 aggregate includes the following components:

(a) notes and coins in circulation with the public,
(b) *plus* private sector interest-bearing and non-interest bearing (sight) sterling bank deposits,
(c) *plus* private sector sterling time bank deposits (with original maturity of up to two years),
(d) *plus* private sector holdings of bank certificates of deposit,
(e) *plus* private sector sterling time bank deposits (original maturity over two years).

Public sector sterling bank deposits are excluded from sterling M3's composition because such deposits are both small and unlikely to influence economic behaviour.

1. The *direct* effect on sterling M3 of an increase in sales of gilt-edged securities by the Bank of England will depend upon who purchases them. If the purchasers are the UK *non-bank* private sector, then sterling M3 will be reduced. This will happen because when the non-bank public make payment to the Bank of England for their security purchases, they will draw cheques on their sight deposits with banks. This will reduce the private sector's non-interest bearing sterling sight deposits with banks. This, in turn, will reduce sterling M3 because these deposits are a component (see component 2, p 57) of sterling M3. If the *banking sector* purchases the gilt-edged securities, then there will be no change in sterling M3. The reason for this is twofold:
    (a) Banking sector purchases of securities reduce the operational deposits of the banking sector with the Bank of England; but the banking sector's operational deposits **are not** a component of sterling M3.
    (b) Banking sector purchases of securities do not affect the bank deposits of the UK non-bank private sector, which **are** a component of sterling M3. The purchases of gilt-edged securities by *overseas residents* will reduce their sterling sight deposits with banks, but these deposits are not included in the components of sterling M3. Hence sterling M3 will not be affected.
2. If the companies pay VAT by drawing cheques on the credit balances in their sterling sight deposits with banks, then sterling M3 will be reduced: 'companies' are a part of the UK private sector, and UK private sector sterling sight deposits with banks are a component of sterling M3. However, if the companies paid their VAT bill by increasing bank borrowing, say, by

overdrawing their sterling sight deposits with banks, then sterling M3 will remain unaffected; the increase in bank lending is offset by a reduction in bank operational balances, so that sterling deposits remain the same.

3. An increase in sterling lending to the overseas sector has the same effect as any bank lending, i.e. a rise in bank deposits. If a rise in bank deposits is 'matched' by an increase in the sterling deposits of overseas residents, then sterling M3 will be unaffected; simply because overseas residents' deposits are not a part of sterling M3. If, however, the overseas residents have increased sterling borrowing in order to meet their commitments to the UK non-bank public, say, in respect of export credits, or the purchase of a business, then the UK private sector sterling deposits with the banks will increase, and so will sterling M3.

A STEP FURTHER

Once again, as with 'Money', your best source for money supply figures and definitions is the *Quarterly Bulletin* of the Bank of England. Articles on money supply matters appear often in the quality newspapers, in *Banking World* and in the *Updating Notes* and *Examiners' Reports* (published by The Institute of Bankers); these are of extreme importance not only to keep abreast of the latest changes in the topic of money supply, but also to see an analysis of the reasons for, and the expected effects of, such changes. More important than the statistics of money supply are the *principles* underlying the concept of money supply.

A Guide to Monetary Policy, published by the Banking Information Service, provides an excellent basic coverage of several aspects of money and money supply.

Chapter 5

Monetary theory and policy

- Have an understanding of monetary economic theory.
- Understand the importance of money as an economic indicator.
- Appreciate the factors which determine the demand for money.
- Outline the Keynesian and monetarist viewpoints on how money influences the economy in relation to the key variables; consumption, savings, investment, interest rates, employment, inflation and the balance of payments.
- Evaluate the different policy implications arising from the Keynesian and monetarist viewpoints.
- Analyse and evaluate the role and techniques of monetary policy.
- Identify the objectives, targets and instruments of policy.
- Assess the effectiveness of monetary policy generally and its relationship to fiscal policy.
- Evaluate the various techniques of monetary policy and the effect of each upon the banking system – interest rate policy, ratios, open market operations, special deposits, quantitative and qualitative controls, suggestion and request.

GETTING STARTED

Monetary policy is a set of measures by which the authorities attempt to regulate the aggregate expenditure in the economy by influencing liquidity and the terms and availability of credit in the country.

There are of course other policies which the authorities may use, either singly or in combination, to regulate aggregate demand in the economy. The authorities may attempt to regulate the level of economic activity by influencing public receipts (i.e. taxes) and public expenditure, (e.g. by using fiscal policy). Alternatively, the authorities may attempt to control the spending ability of the private sector directly, e.g. by pursuing a prices and incomes policy.

The objectives of monetary policy are set within the broad framework of national economic policy, so that the techniques of monetary policy may influence aggregate purchasing power in a manner which is consistent with the broader economic objectives. Such broader economic objectives may be divided into internal and external objectives. Internal objectives might include stable prices, a high employment level, rising economic growth and living standards, and a fair distribution of wealth among individuals, industries and regions of the country. External objectives might include a stable exchange rate for the national currency, a satisfactory balance of payments and level of foreign currency reserves, and the provision of aid to developing countries.

The dilemma that confronts the authorities is that achievement of some of these objectives may clash with the achievement of others. For example, the pursuit of high economic growth and employment may lead to inflationary pressures which may destabilize prices internally. Again, the maintenance of a stable exchange rate externally, may become difficult if inflation internally is making exports less attractive overseas and imports more attractive than domestically produced import substitutes. It is doubtful whether *all* the economic policy objectives can be achieved simultaneously. Hence it is a question, for the authorities, of assigning priorities among the objectives: which of the objectives should be given highest priority will depend upon the needs of the economy at any given period of time.

In recent years, most governments in the free world have faced varying degrees of rising inflation rates, which have undermined the value of people's incomes, savings and profits. Hence the main objective for most governments has been, for several years, 'stable prices', to help money regain and retain its legitimate value, both internally and externally. The belief has been that stable prices will in themselves lead to a higher rate of economic growth and a higher level of employment.

ESSENTIAL PRINCIPLES

Let us assume that the authorities in a 'free' economy decide that the control of inflation is the *broad economic objective* that has highest priority, and that to achieve it, the major *monetary policy objective* is to be the control of expenditure. In the achievement of particular monetary policy objectives, central banks play a pivotal role.

In a free economy, the central bank cannot use monetary policy to control expenditure directly: there is no physical rationing under 'free' economies in normal times. Instead it tries to control expenditure by using indirect methods, such as setting intermediate monetary targets, e.g. controlling the rate of increase in money supply. To control the increase in money supply, it sets operating targets on the banking and financial institutions, e.g. reserve asset requirements to reduce the credit multiplier. To accomplish its various operating targets, the central bank employs a range of monetary instruments, e.g. open market operations or imposing its own interest rates.

There are therefore various stages in the conduct of monetary policy, which are invariably interlinked:

Instruments→Operating targets→Intermediate targets→Monetary policy objective; and of course vice versa.

While the central bank has complete control over its own instruments, which in turn exert control over *operating targets*, yet from then onwards its control becomes gradually weaker. It cannot, for instance, fully control the *intermediate targets*, e.g. the growth of money supply, because the growth of money supply in a free economy depends on the behaviour of banks and their customers. For instance, the central bank has no control over how much credit bank customers demand or banks provide at a given level of interest rate. The link between the *intermediate target* and the *monetary policy objective*, e.g. the control of expenditure, also depends upon the behaviour of the general public: it is the general public which decides how much will be spent from a given amount of money supply available within the economy.

Thus the main issue in monetary policy is how far the things that the central bank *can* control enable it effectively to influence the things it *cannot* control wholly. The more reliable the links between the various stages of the monetary policy, the more successful will the central bank be in achieving the various objectives of monetary policy. We have assumed, for the purposes of analysis, that the *monetary policy objective* is to control expenditure (in order to control inflation). The central bank should then choose as the *intermediate target* that monetary variable which is most reliably linked to expenditure and upon which the central bank can exert most influence. In our analysis we assumed, for illustration, that money supply was such a monetary variable.

MONETARY POLICY TARGETS

There are five main variables from which the central bank, observing the above criteria, may choose intermediate targets in order to control expenditure: (1) The Money Supply; (2) Credit; (3) Interest Rates; (4) Exchange Rates; (5) Expenditure.

The money supply

The monetarists think that money supply is a good intermediate target. They believe that increases in money supply will, via the 'transmission mechanism', increase expenditure, some of the new money being used to buy goods and services, which increases expenditure directly, and some being invested in safe securities, such as first-class fixed-interest bonds, which increases expenditure indirectly. Buying bonds increases the market prices of such bonds but lowers interest rates: lower interest rates increase investment and consumption expenditure. Hence, the monetarists argue, the central bank should choose the growth in money supply as the intermediate target when it seeks to control expenditure.

There are some problems in making money supply growth the intermediate target for controlling expenditure.

1. Income and expenditure are identities: A's income is B's expenditure. If Y = income and M = money supply, then $Y = Mk$, where k is the velocity of circulation of money, i.e. the average number of times each unit of money is received as income. For example, if $Y = 100$ and $M = 50$, then $k = 2$. The behaviour of k is the crucial link between money supply and expenditure, and clearly a reduction in M could still be consistent with an increase in expenditure if k were to increase. The size of k will, in fact, depend upon the demand for money in the economy: with a given stock of money, M, the greater the demand to hold money, the *lower* will be k, and therefore the lower will be the level of income and expenditure. The demand for money is generally dependent upon the level of income *and* the level of interest rates (see Ch. 6). The more income people have, the more money they will want to hold as a means of payment in order to finance transactions; but the higher the rate of interest (rate of return) on other financial assets, the lower the demand to hold money. Generally, an increase in income will raise the demand to hold money, but an increase in interest rates will lower the demand to hold money.

2. Another problem arises with regard to how interest-elastic is the demand for money. Suppose firms decide to increase investment, while money stock is stationary; this will raise interest rates which, in turn, will lower the demand to hold money and increase its velocity of circulation. Therefore higher levels of both income and expenditure will be possible with no increase in money stock.

   The extent to which the change in velocity upsets the relationship between money, income and expenditure will depend upon how interest-elastic is the demand for money. If the demand for money is, as monetarists believe, interest-inelastic, then any change in interest rates will cause a small change in velocity, so that money, income and expenditure may still have quite a close relationship.

   In any case, the central bank could reduce the *rate* of monetary growth to compensate for any increase in velocity. This, however, would involve the central bank in doing two very difficult things: first, *estimating* fairly closely the extent of the reduction in the demand for money (increase in velocity), and second, judging whether this reduction is temporary or likely to continue – if it misjudges, it could make things worse rather than better by reducing the rate of money supply growth. Besides, cutting the rate of monetary growth will not have its full effect on expenditure until the private sector has had time to adjust its expenditure pattern to it. The danger then is that, if the level of private sector expenditure does not decrease to the expected level, an impatient central bank may *further* reduce money so that, in due course, the twin action of a double reduction of money supply growth may create undesirable fluctuations in expenditure.

Thus for money supply to be a useful intermediate target, it is essential that the velocity of circulation of money is reasonably stable. This in turn, will depend upon whether the demand for money is interest-elastic or inelastic. The velocity of circulation of money will be more stable the more interest-inelastic is the demand for money.

Assuming that the monetary authorities decide to make money supply an intermediate target, they then will need to make further decisions in respect to the following:

(a) Which monetary aggregate should they choose as a target? Most central banks monitor a range of narrow and broad monetary targets, which include a widening range of financial assets on the liquidity spectrum. Each central bank would choose that monetary aggregate as a target which is most closely related to expenditure and over which it has the most control.

(b) Having chosen the monetary aggregate, should the authorities publicly announce it? If the public believed that the central bank would be able to achieve the target, and that this achievement would cut inflation, then the public, including trade unions, might accept lower future money incomes, without anticipating a fall in their 'real' income and therefore in their standards of living. Business firms would then require lower price increases to achieve a particular level of 'real' profitability. These are some of the advantages of publicly announcing the targets and their growth rates. However, a disadvantage of such announcement would be to curtail the authorities' flexibility of action. The authorities would not be able to change the targets for the monetary aggregate without being accused of a 'U'-turn, even though changes in economic conditions might require such changes in targets.

(c) Should there be point targets or target ranges? While precise point targets reduce uncertainty in the minds of the public, they are also very difficult to achieve, especially during a fluctuating economic climate. Therefore, it would probably be more realistic to set a target range, e.g. 7–10 per cent per annum growth rate; this would also allow some flexibility of action to the authorities.

Credit

In modern economies, credit (bank lending) and money are closely linked. An increase in bank lending usually leads to an increase in bank deposits and therefore an increase in money supply. As modern societies become more and more 'cashless', the role of bank lending becomes crucial to aggregate expenditure in the economy.

The volume of bank lending is however determined not only by the banks but also by the overall demand for credit in the economy. The immediate effect of a rise in total bank credit will be to increase bank deposits, but some of the increase in deposits may disappear if the borrowers substitute, say, government bonds for their bank deposits; in this case, government accounts with the central bank will increase and the banking sector's balances with the central bank and their share of total deposits will fall by the same amount. It is when the public buy more of other financial assets, using their bank deposits, that the total stock of bank deposits will be reduced. The volume of bank lending will also be determined by the amount of competition from *non-bank lenders*.

If Bank A, by taking positive action – higher deposit rate, better services, greater liquidity, etc. – attracts deposits away from *other banks*, they will need to draw upon their operational balances with the central bank. Thus this transfer of deposits from other banks to Bank A will not reduce or increase the total stock of bank deposits.

Is credit (bank lending) a good intermediate target? Although money supply and bank credit are closely linked, and a rise in bank credit is one of the ways in which money supply and therefore expenditure may increase, yet there is no reason why money supply and bank lending should grow at the same time or at the same rate: if banks increase lending to the public, but at the same time the central bank sells securities to the public, then there is no increase in money supply, even though bank lending has increased.

Some economists argue that credit is a better intermediate target than money supply in controlling expenditure, because households and firms rarely borrow unless they wish to spend. Therefore, an increase in credit should have a predictable effect on expenditure, and the control of credit should, more predictably, control expenditure. However, *if* credit is taken as an intermediate target of monetary policy, then *all* credit should be the basis for the control of expenditure by the authorities – bank credit *plus* funds borrowed by the public from non-bank financial institutions.

Interest rates

If the authorities knew reasonably well what level of expenditure would result from a given level of interest rates, then interest rates would be a possible candidate for the intermediate target. However, the problem with interest rates as a target is that it is the *expectations* of businessmen, and not interest rates, which determine expenditure by firms. If business expectations of future demand and profitability rise considerably, then firms will increase their borrowing of investment funds, no matter what the level of interest rates. Even if the authorities do stabilize interest rates, at any given level of interest rates, the level of expenditure may fluctuate widely, due to sudden changes in business expectations. Furthermore, 'distress borrowing' of the non-bank public is interest-inelastic. Therefore interest rates may have a poor correlation with credit and/or money supply, and an unreliable link with expenditure.

Exchange rates

The exchange rate is the price of domestic currency in terms of foreign currencies. In those economies in which international trade accounts for a relatively high proportion of economic activity, changes in exchange rates can cause considerable disturbance in the domestic economy. For example, a fall in exchange rates will make exports more, and imports less, competitive, which will stimulate domestic economic activity; if the exchange rate rises, the reverse will happen, and domestic economic activity will be depressed.

If the country has a fixed exchange rate as its intermediate target, but has a higher domestic inflation rate than that of its trading partners, then the competitiveness of its exports will suffer, leading to pressure for a devaluation of its exchange rate to such an extent as would neutralize the inflation rate differentials.

While the authorities, by intervening directly (through selling foreign or domestic currency) or by manipulating domestic interest rates (see Ch. 8), can influence the exchange rate of the domestic currency, a country's foreign currency reserves, or its ability to borrow currency overseas, are not limitless. Hence direct official intervention can only be to a limited extent; and manipulation of interest rates beyond certain levels may have dangerous effects for the economy. This could happen if external pressures lead to higher domestic interest rates than domestic conditions might warrant.

Expenditure

The authorities could choose expenditure itself as an intermediate target to control inflation; however, if they did so, two major problems would confront them. First, there is a time lag, often of up to two years, before expenditure by households and firms responds fully to changes in monetary policy; impatient monetary authorities might change the monetary policy *before* the full effects of the current monetary policy had become apparent. Second, since current information on the growth of expenditure is not readily available, the authorities could be seriously handicapped in their monetary policy decisions for lack of up-to-date information on expenditure growth.

INSTRUMENTS AND METHODS OF MONETARY CONTROL

The two main components of money supply in modern economies are cash (notes and coins) and deposits with banks and non-bank financial institutions. Central banks do not normally control the supply of cash in circulation; this is determined by the preference of the public for cash or deposits; there can, for instance, be large seasonal variations in the public preference for cash or deposits. Central banks, however, attempt to regulate, in several ways, the growth of total deposits, but especially the growth of bank deposits, because these deposits constitute a significant proportion of the total money supply.

The following methods or techniques (instruments) are commonly used by the central bank to control the level of bank deposits (operating target).

1. Direct controls

This technique places direct restrictions on bank lending or deposit growth. There are two instruments of direct control, lending ceilings and direct interest rate control.

Lending ceilings

The central bank instructs the commercial banks not to lend above a prescribed ceiling, say 6 per cent per annum. Since the commercial banks have to abide by the direct instructions of the central bank, the main advantage of of this instrument is that bank lending, and therefore bank deposits, will not increase beyond 6 per cent per annum. As against this advantage, there are two serious disadvantages:

(a) Unless the lending ceilings are applied uniformly to *all* lending institutions, the borrowing public could quite easily switch that part of its borrowing requirements which are *in excess* of the bank lending ceilings to uncontrolled non-bank lending institutions; then disintermediation, with all its distorting effects on money supply, would occur.
(b) Competition and innovation among banks would be inhibited to the detriment of bank customers.

2. Direct interest rate control

On the assumption that the public's demand for funds is interest-elastic, the central bank requires commercial banks to charge such rates as would influence public borrowing according to money supply growth targets; setting a higher rate to decrease bank lending, and a lower rate to increase it. Direct interest controls can however cause several complications:

(a) Unless interest rate control is uniformly applied to all lending institutions, 'round tripping' or arbitrage could be triggered: if controlled rates are below uncontrolled rates, the non-bank public could borrow cheaply at controlled rates and lend the borrowed sum, at a quick profit, at uncontrolled rates. Round tripping leads to a misallocation of funds.
(b) The size of the PSBR is determined by the government's tax revenue and spending policy; *public sector borrowing* is largely interest-inelastic and therefore insensitive to interest rate controls.
(c) *Private sector borrowing* is not always interest-elastic. The possibility of profitable investment may be related more to business expectation than to the level of interest rate. 'Distress' borrowings are also largely unrelated to interest rates.
(d) Direct interest rate control has a delayed, or lagged, effect on bank lending: this is because the expenditure commitments of firms and households take time to adjust to changed interest rates. It may therefore be just when the non-bank public has begun to adjust its borrowing requirements in line with the objective of controlled interest rates, that the central bank may decide to alter the level of the controlled rates again.
(e) Rigid interest rate control may clash with other economic policy objectives, e.g. a rigidly applied high interest rate policy may militate against the need to increase investment in order to counteract rising unemployment.

Open market operations of the central bank

Open market operations are a two-way weapon in the armoury of the central bank. On a day-to-day basis the technique is used to smooth out fluctuations in liquidity in the money market. This means the central bank selling money market instruments to mop up excess liquidity, and buying these instruments to relieve any liquidity shortage in the market. This type of open market operation will be applied at the existing interest rate level.

However, if the authorities wish interest rates to change, then the central bank will do so by buying and selling money market instruments at a rate higher or lower than is consistent with the existing interest rate level. Sometimes the central bank may deliberately create a shortage of liquidity in the money market by selling excessively attractive government and money market instruments, and then relieve the shortage at its own terms; this will raise the level of money market interest rates.

Cash-to-deposit ratio and reserve asset ratio requirements

Both these requirements place constraints on the commercial banks' asset structure. If the central bank requires them to maintain, say, a 20 per cent cash-to-deposit ratio, it will clearly reduce their ability to lend by 20 per cent. If the central bank now requires that a portion of their cash-to-deposit ratio should be kept in specified reserve assets, so that the reserve asset ratio falls below the required level, the banks will either have to curtail lending by raising lending rates, or have to bid for more deposits (by raising deposit rates or converting their non-reserve assets into reserve assets). The effect of imposing these requirements is to reduce the credit multiplier.

Monetary base control (see Ch. 4)

The real source of spending money for the general public is the money base, i.e. the operational balances of the commercial banks with the central bank; therefore, by controlling the money base, the central bank should be able to control the availability of spending money. However, the problem is that if MBC is rigidly applied, it may trigger off violent fluctuations in interest rates and thereby cause disintermediation. The key to the success of MBC is that the assets of the monetary base on which the credit multiplier is pivoted must be *completely* in the control of the central bank. This is not always possible, for the reasons considered in Chapter 4.

FISCAL AND MONETARY POLICIES

The word 'fiscal' comes from the Latin 'fiscus', meaning pertaining to the public treasury, i.e. the income or revenue of a state. Thus fiscal policy implies management of aggregate demand in the economy by varying the size and the content of public revenue (i.e. taxes) and government expenditure, and making good any deficit by borrowing.

The objectives of fiscal policy, within the wider framework of economic policy, are:

1. Internal – to achieve a high level of employment; to promote economic growth and increase national income; to bring about a fair distribution of wealth and resources among individuals, industries and regions; to protect vital and infant industries against foreign competition, and to raise the living standards of the population.

2.   External – to achieve a satisfactory balance of payments and to defend the foreign exchange value of the national currency.

In order to achieve these objectives, the authorities act by varying the size and direction of government spending, the size and composition of public revenue – mainly by alterations in direct and indirect taxes – and the size and sources of government borrowing.

The Public Sector Borrowing Requirement (PSBR) is the excess of public sector spending over public sector revenue. It is generally financed by borrowing from the banks and non-banks. If it is financed mainly by *banks* in exchange for government securities, then the banks will be able to use these securities to increase their deposits, and the money supply will increase. On the other hand, if the PSBR is to be financed by the *non-bank* public, then the yields (interest rate returns) on the government bonds (securities) will have to be raised sufficiently high to attract the public to buy the government bonds. High interest rates will tend to curb investment and consumption expenditure. Thus, fiscal policy measures cannot be implemented independently of monetary policy measures. However, monetary policy can be implemented by the authorities independently of fiscal policy: the central bank can alter its lending rate and/or issue instructions to commercial banks on their lending activities, thereby putting into motion the desired changes in the growth of the money supply and in the general level of interest rates.

POLICY IMPLICATIONS

The Keynesian view

Keynesians agree that monetary policy measures – control of money supply and interest rates – will affect the aggregate expenditure in the economy. However, they doubt whether the extent of the effect of these measures would be sufficient to control investment and consumption expenditures. They seriously doubt that controlling money supply will have a sufficiently strong and rapid impact on the level of expenditure. Any effect the level of money might have on expenditure would tend to be indirect, through changes in interest rates. An increase in money supply would lower interest rates and encourage an increase in investment and consumption expenditures; this would then help the economy to move up from recession. Conversely, a reduction in money supply would raise interest rates, discourage aggregate expenditure and put the brakes on an overheated economy, which would then help reduce inflation.

The Keynesians therefore support a monetary policy which is directed towards influencing the level of interest rates *directly*, and not indirectly via money supply. However, even with interest rates as the monetary policy objective, they do not feel too confident, because they doubt whether the interest-elasticity of investment and consumption expenditure is sufficiently sensitive to change aggregate expenditure to its desired level. Thus they advocate *aggregate demand management* by fiscal policy measure, i.e. changes in the PSBR. For instance, if the economy is caught up in a deep recession, and private aggregate expenditure is unable, or unwilling, to pull it out of recession, then the government should lead the way by appropriately increasing public expenditure year by year, for a period of years. The increases in public expenditure will have an income 'multiplier' effect, i.e. an exaggerated effect on income in the economy: any increase in the incomes of workers in one sector of the economy will, as it is spent, become the income of workers in other sectors in the economy, and so on, because income and expenditure are identities. Conversely, a budget surplus – excess of public revenue over public expenditure – would make use of the income multiplier in reverse; for instance, to bring about a rapid deceleration of an overheated economy, thereby controlling inflation. It is the management of aggregate demand, via fiscal policy, which is at the heart of the Keynesian policy prescription.

The monetarists' view

Monetarists strongly believe that increases in money supply increase incomes, and vice versa. Since the velocity of circulation of money, and total output, are both assumed to be fairly stable, any increase in income leads to increased expenditure, which then leads to inflationary increases in prices. If the money supply still continues to increase then inflation will become rampant in the economy.

High inflation damages the economy in various ways: real incomes fall, leading to demand for higher wages; a fall in returns on investment leads to demand for higher interest rates; higher interest rates reduce aggregate investment and increase unemployment; higher prices internally discourage exports and encourage imports, and therefore the balance of payments suffers; business uncertainty increases. Since the cumulation of the high inflation rate, with its attendant 'evil' effects, is caused by increases in money supply over a number of years, to unwind the effects of a high inflation rate, the money supply growth rate should be decreased over a number of years, until inflation has been squeezed out of the economy. Once inflation has been brought under control, and the public believe that the authorities will not let it escalate again, business confidence will recover, encouraged by lower interest rates and by lower wage settlements. These will stimulate investment, exports and employment. Once the inflation is brought under control, then the authorities may provide for controlled growth in the money supply, to promote economic growth and to generate an increase in real incomes.

With the above belief, the monetarists advocate a monetary policy objective of controlling the rate of growth of the money supply; continuous reduction in money supply growth will create expectations within business firms, trade unions and the general public that the monetary authorities are determined in their resolve to win the battle against inflation. To create such expectations in the country, the authorities should announce their monetary targets for several years in advance.

Monetarist beliefs and policy objectives are seriously criticized by some economists. The main criticisms are, firstly, that the monetarists are incorrect in believing that the velocity of circulation of money is stable, and, secondly, that the link between money supply and aggregate expenditure is too variable to justify the monetarists' emphasis on money supply control. If there is high unemployment and large spare capacity in the economy, then increases in money supply will increase output, not prices, at least until full employment of resources has been reached; therefore, more important than money supply control are the direct controls on prices and/or incomes, i.e. a Prices and Incomes Policy. Critics also argue that the social costs of bringing down inflation by reducing money supply growth over a number of years, in the shape of massive unemployment, are too high compared to the benefits of lower inflation.

USEFUL APPLIED MATERIALS

MONETARY POLICY IN BRITAIN

By 1973, control over the growth of money supply had become the main objective of the monetary authorities. In 1976, the official practice of announcing targets for money supply growth was started, and since then the authorities have tried gradually to reduce the rate of growth of money supply. Successive governments attached greater importance to the intermediate target of controlling the growth of money supply, believing this to be vital in containing inflation. This gave monetary policy the prominence previously accorded to fiscal policy.

From 1976 to 1981 sterling M3 was considered by the authorities to be the most important monetary target, mainly because of the clear relationship between it and its counterparts. Therefore, from 1976 to 1981, 'target ranges' were announced in sterling M3 only. Successive monetary authorities, to allow themselves some flexibility, have set target ranges, and not point targets, for sterling M3 growth. In order to control the growth of the money supply progressively, these targets have been gradually reduced. This policy of monetary control was designed to limit private sector demand in the economy, particularly by influencing private sector expectations as to future inflation; hence the monetary targets have been publicly announced in advance.

However, these target ranges have been frequently exceeded. The reason for this lies in the difficulty confronted by the monetary authorities in controlling money supply. If the Bank of England were to use changes in interest rates to control money supply, then it had to estimate fairly precisely the total demand for credit by the private sector at various levels of interest rate. The Bank in fact underestimated the private firms' demand for credit in 1979 and 1980. Again, if the exchange rate is too high and attracts hot money, then domestic interest rates will need to be lowered; but lowering interest rates will increase money supply! This was the cause of the sterling M3 target being exceeded in 1977/78. Yet again, the level of interest rates required to keep the exchange rate at a particular level may well be different from the level of interest rates required to meet the money supply growth target. Since changes in the exchange rate have significant effects on the rate of domestic inflation and on economic activity, the authorities gave priority to the control of the exchange rate during 1976 to 1981, at the expense of the sterling M3 targets.

In 1981, the authorities were getting a little disenchanted with sterling M3 as the sole monetary target setter. This was largely due to certain factors outside the control of the authorities, e.g. the effects on the money supply of unwinding the 'corset'; this gave rise to disintermediation and therefore distorted the money supply, being reflected in the sterling M3 figures. Therefore, from March 1982 until March 1984, the authorities announced *multiple* monetary target ranges in terms of sterling M3, M1 and PSL2. In March 1984 the multiple target range was announced in terms of M0, 4 to 8 per cent (due to deficiencies in M1 as a narrow money aggregate), and sterling M3, 6 to 10 per cent. In the March 1985 budget the multiple target ranges for 1985/86 were set at 3 to7 per cent (M0) and 5 to 9 per cent (sterling M3). However, in October 1985 the Chancellor announced the abandonment of sterling M3 as a target and, therefore, the authorities will no longer seek to control its growth by systematic overfunding, i.e. selling gilt stocks in excess of the PSBR requirements. The reason for the abandonment is that sterling M3 is now rising at an annual rate of 18.5%, way above the limit set by the Chancellor in the 1985 budget.

Monetary policy has not been used for short-term demand management, i.e. there have been no changes in monetary targets to offset short-term fluctuations in demand and inflation. Rather the authorities have sought to control the growth of money supply on a year-to-year basis in order to limit the build-up of demand and inflationary pressures.

There is no official exchange rate target in the UK monetary policy; however, since the January 1985 sterling crisis (when sterling fell sharply and interest rates had to be raised by 4½ per cent to 14 per cent to half its fall), the exchange rate has been apparently assigned an elevated role in the UK monetary policy.

MEDIUM TERM FINANCIAL STRATEGY (MTFS)

Broadly speaking, the government employs fiscal policy in support of its monetary policy objectives, e.g. reducing public sector borrowing and spending in order to reduce money supply and thereby interest rates. The present government has sought to restrain the public sector's demand for funds in order to achieve its monetary targets at lower interest rates, and thus to encourage more domestic investment and output in the private sector. The combined objectives for money supply **and** public sector borrowing were first established in 1980, and are known collectively as the Medium Term Financial Strategy.

In 1980, MTFS was introduced by the authorities. It sets monetary plans, as distinct from annual targets, for a number of years ahead, including those for public spending and tax policies. The basic aims of MTFS are to reduce inflation and to transfer more resources to the private sector. The reasoning underlying the MTFS objectives is that a higher PSBR requires higher interest rates to finance it, resulting in higher inflation. The suggestion is that public sector borrowing tends to be interest-inelastic, whereas private sector borrowing trends to be more sensitive to higher interest rates. Therefore the higher interest rates required to meet the increased needs of the public sector borrowing requirement 'crowds out' private sector expenditure; this arrests economic growth and employment.

In 1980, the MTFS plans for growth of sterling M3 and for the PSBR as a percentage of the National Income were announced. These plans showed a planned fall for both the growth of sterling M3 and for the PSBR as a percentage of National Income. However, these plans had to be revised in 1983, because monetary targets were heavily exceeded and the PSBR had been higher than projected; the latter being due to a deeper than expected recession, resulting in lower tax revenue than anticipated, and higher spending on unemployment and other welfare benefits.

CURRENT MONETARY CONTROL TECHNIQUES IN THE UK

The monetary policy in the UK is designed, in the main, to control money supply, interest rates and the exchange rate of the pound sterling. Until 1980, the authorities used several control techniques, such as reserve asset ratio requirements, quantitative and qualitative controls on bank lending, Minimum Lending Rate changes, open market operations, and calls for special deposits. Of these control techniques, only open market operations, the possibility of resurrecting the Minimum Lending Rate, calls for special deposits and 'qualitative guidance' (requests by the Bank of England to banks that they give priority in lending to certain sectors of the economy, and restrain lending to other sectors) have survived the 1981 changes.

Open market operations involve the buying and selling by the Bank of England of commercial and Treasury bills to influence:

(a) the cash and liquidity base of the banking system and therefore the capacity of banks to lend;
(b) directly the level of short-term interest rates and indirectly the structure of longer-term interest rates.

If the objective of open market operations is to *affect the growth of bank advances* in order to control the growth in money supply, then the Bank relieves the liquidity shortage in the market at a bill dealing rate which is higher than the current money market rate. In this way the Bank is able to control the marginal cost of funds to the banking system. The level of short-term (up to three months) inter-bank rates broadly corresponds to the marginal cost of banks' funds. However, since the Bank in its OMOs continues to deal primarily with the discount houses, its bill dealing rates can be out of line with interbank rates; the difference between the two rates represents the marginal cost of funds to the commercial banks. The level of banks' base rates tends to move in line with money market rates. A rise in the banks' base rates, the authorities believe, would lower the demand for bank lending and, in turn, would curb the growth in money supply.

If the objective of the OMOs is simply to *relieve any shortage or surplus of liquid funds* in the money market, then the Bank buys and sells money market instruments at a bill dealing rate that is equal to the existing level of short-term interest rates.

If the authorities wish to encourage the public to hold the public sector debt for a longer term, they will attempt to affect the *structure* of interest rates. While changes in the Bank's bill dealing rates will directly affect the level of short-term rates, these changes will also indirectly affect the structure of longer-term rates; they will do this by affecting market expectations as to the movements in longer-term rates, e.g. movement of short-term rates over the year (yield curve) will influence the one-year money market rate.

The open market operations are conducted by the Bank of England exclusively in the bill market via the discount houses, and in order to ensure an adquate supply of commercial bills – bills of exchange issued by commercial firms to finance short-term transactions – the authorities have increased the number of eligible banks, i.e. banks whose acceptances the Bank is prepared to rediscount. As a condition of eligibility, and the status that goes with eligibility, the Bank requires each eligible bank to maintain, on average, secured interest-bearing money with the discount houses and/or with money brokers and gilt-edged jobbers, equal to 5 per cent of its deposits; the proportion held with the discount houses should not fall below $2\frac{1}{2}$ per cent of its deposits on any day. All institutions in the monetary sector are obliged to keep with the Bank $\frac{1}{2}$ per cent of their deposits in non-operational and non-interest bearing deposits. This requirement is not meant to affect the assets of the banks – although it does; rather, it is meant to provide the Bank with operational balances to assist it in its open market operations.

Under the 'dirty' floating exchange rate policy pursued in the UK, the authorities seek to hold the exchange rate of sterling within a range which they believe to be in the best interests of the economy as a whole. To prevent the exchange rate falling dangerously low, the Bank of England will seek to raise short-term interest rates respectively to reduce the supply of, and increase the demand for, sterling on the foreign exchange markets.

The effectiveness of monetary control in the UK has not been an unqualified success.

As far as the *manipulation of interest rates* is concerned, via open market operations, the interest rate policy has suffered due to two reasons.

1. The Bank of England cannot control *both* the money supply and the price of money, i.e. interest rates, simultaneously:
2. The demand for bank advances, at least in the short-run, is often interest-inelastic.

The *control of money supply* through reserve requirements and other direct quantitative controls on bank lending have encouraged disintermediation, leading to the growth of lending and of financial assets outside the controlled banking system. In such circumstances, the money supply only *appears* to be under the control of the authorities.

The attempts by the Bank of England to ease the acute downward pressure on the *foreign exchange value of sterling* by raising the level of short-term interest rates has attracted excessive inflow of foreign speculative and investment balances into the country. This has had adverse effects on efforts to control the growth of money supply.

The above analysis of the problems and after-effects of monetary policy which has sought to control interest rates, the money supply, and the exchange rate, shows that the authorities cannot, in practice, achieve the intermediate monetary target of controlling all these variables *at the same time*, however much they might think otherwise.

RECENT EXAMINATION QUESTIONS

The following six questions have been asked in recent years on the topic of monetary policy and its relationship with fiscal policy. Before looking at the outline answers, spend ten minutes or so trying to identify the main points to be used in your answer to each question.

Question 1.

To what extent is a successful anti-inflationary policy necessarily associated with an increase in unemployment? Illustrate your answer with reference to the economic experience of the UK during the past decade.

Question 2.

(a) Outline the principal goals of economic policy.
(b) Consider the extent to which monetary policy in the UK has been successful in achieving these economic goals in recent years.

Question 3.

'Monetary targets are pretty meaningless unless a *broad* definition is used.' (Kaldor and Trevithick, 1981). In the light of this statement, discuss the problems which have occurred in the implementation of the UK monetary policy.

Question 4.

Outline the main changes in monetary control techniques that have occurred in the United Kingdom during 1980 and 1981. How have these changes affected the commercial banks?

Question 5.

Compare and contrast the 'monetarist' and Keynesian viewpoint of how an increase in a country's money supply affects growth, inflation and the level of interest rates. Distinguish between short- and long-term effects.

Question 6.

Discuss the view that it is possible to control either the money supply or the level of interest rates, but not both. What practical implication does this view have for the way in which the monetary authorities seek to control the money supply?

OUTLINE ANSWERS

Answer 1.

(a) Explain alternative policies to control inflation:

- Deflation: via monetary policy and/or fiscal policy.
- Prices and incomes policy: to control aggregate demand and expenditure.

- Import controls: their effects on balance of payments deficit.
(b) Discuss causes of inflation:
- Cost-push: increased labour costs pushing up prices.
- Demand-pull: prices pulled up by too much money chasing too few goods.
(c) Outline the viewpoints on control of inflation in the UK of:
- Keynesians: trade-off between inflation and unemployment.
- Monetarists: no trade-off between inflation and unemployment.

Answer 2.

(a) List clearly the traditional goals of economic policy:
- Full employment; stable prices; slight surplus in the current account of balance of payments; reasonable 'real' economic growth rate; satisfactory and stable exchange rate; a more equal distribution of income, between rich and poor people or between rich and poor areas.
(b) Explain the problems confronted by the authorities in achieving all goals simultaneously:
- Inherent conflicts among goals: control of inflation leads to rising unemployment and unsatisfactory exchange rate.
- Monetary policy, like fiscal policy, is an integral part of economic policy, and is not easy to isolate for analysis.
- MTFS and its link with PSBR and money supply.

Answer 3.

(a) The key word is 'monetary', not 'economic'.
(b) State monetary targets (in 1981), with working definitions: M1, sterling M3, PSL2.
(c) State and analyse the problems in implementing monetary policy in 1981.
- As authorities pulled the corset harder, companies and their bankers found loopholes:
  (i) 'hard' and 'soft' arbitrage;
  (ii) disintermediation: surplus firms, by-passed financial intermediaries, lent to deficit firms by drawing bills or on the inter-company market – money supply statistics distorted;
  (iii) unwinding of corset and civil servants' (Inland Revenue) strike artificially increased money supply figures.
- PSBR increased (deepening recession, rising unemployment and defence costs) which led to increase in money supply (that portion of PSBR not financed by non-bank public).
- High interest rates and high exchange rate (North Sea oil revenue) caused commercial firms to suffer loss of exports, cash flow problems, increased borrowing from banks – bank deposits increased, so did sterling M3, which overshot the 6 to 10 per cent annual target range.
- Bank of England, as a monopolist, can either control money supply or cost of money (interest rates), not both.

Answer 4.

(a) Principal changes in monetary control techniques during 1980 and 1981:
  - *During 1980*: abolition of the 'corset' (actually 1979); phasing out of direct 'lender of last resort' lending by the Bank of England and the use of open market operations in the commercial bill market as an indirect method.
  - *During 1981*: suspension of MLR; Bank of England to keep very short-term interest rates within an unpublished band; 1½ per cent cash ratio on London clearers abolished; ½ per cent cash ratio applied to all banks in the new monetary sector; all 'eligible' banks must keep secured loans, 4 to 6 per cent (now 2½ to 5 per cent) with discount houses; creation of many new eligible banks.

(b) Effects of the above changes on commercial banks:
  - Abandonment of corset: freer lending, visibly in mortgage field.
  - Suspension of MLR: more flexible interest rates, with implication for bank base rates and the pricing of overdrafts.
  - Emphasis by the Bank of England on intervention in the bill markets: upsurge in the use of commercial bill finance and keen competition on 'acceptances' from the new banks.
  - Abolition of the reserve asset ratio: implication for bank balance sheets, able to assess liquidity requirements on prudential grounds in conjunction with the Bank of England.

Answer 5.

(a) The monetarist viewpoint:
  - In the short run: increase in money supply will lower interest rates, raise prices and possibly raise output.
  - In the long run: all increase in money supply absorbed in higher prices with no effect on output; interest rates will be higher, reflecting the higher inflation rate.

(b) The Keynesian viewpoint:
  - Increase in money supply lowers interest rates, which stimulates demand and may result in lasting output growth, rather than in higher inflation, provided the economy has some spare capacity.
  - $P = \dfrac{MV}{T}$

    (M = money, V = velocity of circulation of money, P = price level, T = volume of transactions) – the quantity equation.

Answer 6.

(a) Compare the monetary authorities to a monopolist: he can either control the 'quantity' (the money supply) or the 'price' (the interest rates), but not both.

(b) Implications of above on monetary authorities' controlling of money supply:
  - Selling government securities will be successful if they pay the right 'price' (pay attractive interest on securities).

- The higher the PSBR, the higher the interest rates.
- Monetary base control: authorities should have more direct control on money supply by directly controlling the cash and reserves of the banking system, leaving interest rates to be determined by the market forces.
- Authorities unwilling to abdicate key control over interest rates, therefore willing to provide banking system with the cash and reserves it needs.
- But if money supply rising too fast, authorities forced to raise interest rates either to restrain growth in bank lending and/or encourage purchases of government debt.

A TUTOR'S ANSWER

The following question deals with the theory and the practice of monetary policy. The specimen answer covers the full scope of the question. Try to make a relevant answer plan yourself before reading the specimen answer.

Question

Distinguish between Keynesian and monetarist viewpoints on the motives for holding money. Why are these different approaches of importance for the conduct of monetary policy?

Answer plan
1. Avoid a rambling approach; the question is to be answered by bankers not economists. Be specific and to the point.
2. Outline the Keynesian motives for holding money.
3. Outline the monetarists' viewpoints for holding money.
4. Distinguish between the two approaches.
5. Conclude by showing the impact of the two approaches on the conduct of monetary policy by monetary authorities.
6. Stop, when you have covered the above points.

Specimen answer

The traditional Keynesian motives for holding money (liquidity) are:

(a) transaction motive – real money is needed for day-to-day expenses by households and firms;
(b) precautionary motive – money is held in liquid form to meet unforeseen contingencies;
(c) speculative motive – real money is held to take advantage of changes in interest rates, and therefore in rates of returns on bonds (fixed interest securities).

The key motive is the speculative motive, because it sees money as a substitute for bonds: it means that the demand for money to hold (liquidity preference) will be influenced by changes in interest rates.

The basic monetarist viewpoint on holding money is developed in the quantity theory of money ($MV = PT$, when M = money in circulation, V = velocity of circulation of money, P = general price level, T = total transactions). The quantity theory approach concentrates on the transaction motive, with money viewed as a 'temporary abode of purchasing power'. Modern monetarist theory approaches the demand for money from the point of money being *one* of a number of ways of holding wealth; the other ways include holding equities (ordinary shares), physical assets (e.g. houses), as well as bonds.

The key differences between the Keynesian and monetarist viewpoints is that the Keynesian approach emphasizes money as a substitute for other financial assets, whereas the monetarists see money as a substitute for *both* financial and physical assets.

For the Keynesians, an increase in money supply would mean that the extra money – surplus to transaction and precautionary needs – would be invested in *bonds*, driving up their market prices, and therefore reducing interest rates: bond prices and interest rates are inversely related. What happens next depends on how interest-elastic is the demand for money in the economy. If the demand for money is highly sensitive to a reduction in interest rates, then money held for transaction and precautionary needs will need to be supplemented. Little of the initial *extra* money supply will now be surplus to demand, and available to drive bond prices up still further. In other words, the fall in interest rates will be restricted, doing little to boost consumption and investment (i.e. aggregate demand).

For the monetarists, the effect of an increase in money supply is more widespread, because excess money spills over, not just in the bond market, but into *all* markets; it therefore affects expenditure and demand in the economy as a whole in a more direct way.

The distinction between the two viewpoints is therefore important to the effects on the economy of changes in money supply. According to Keynesians, money supply changes affect the economy indirectly, via interest rate changes. According to monetarists, the effect of changes in money on the economy is more direct.

The Keynesians, while admitting a relationship between money supply changes and interest rate changes, have traditionally held that the effects of interest rate changes on the economy are weak. Therefore the extreme Keynesians suggest the pursuit of fiscal policy (public spending, revenue and borrowing) in preference to monetary policy, for regulating the economy; they believe fiscal policy measures to be a more powerful and effective means of regulating aggregate demand.

The monetarists, on the other hand, staunchly believe that controlling the money supply is the most influential factor in controlling expenditure and demand in the economy, and that fiscal policy at best could have only a temporary effect on the real economy.

Thus, if monetary authorities are wedded to the monetarist viewpoint, they would aim their monetary policy objective towards controlling the money supply by changes in the public sector borrowing requirements (excess of public spending over public revenue). If, on the other hand, the authorities favour the Keynesian viewpoint, then they will use fiscal policy in regulating aggregate demand in the economy, using monetary policy as an adjunct to fiscal policy.

A STEP FURTHER

This chapter and the chapters on 'Money', 'Money Supply' and 'Interest Rates' are closely connected. It is essential for you to understand this linkage in order to gain an overall understanding of domestic monetary economics. The Institute of Bankers' Examiner's *Reports, Updating Notes* and 'signpost' articles in the *Banking World* are extremely useful sources for keeping abreast of various movements in monetary policy, and also in topics linked to monetary policy. In this connection, a study of *A Guide to Monetary Policy*, published by the Banking Information Service, is strongly recommended.

Chapter 6

Interest rates

- Appreciate the significance of interest rates.
- Define the role of the rate of interest and distinguish between real and nominal rates.
- Examine the factors which determine the level and pattern of interest rates.
- Be aware of the structure of interest rates and of important indicators, e.g. LIBOR, overnight rates, base rates, etc.
- Be able to distinguish between short-term and long-term interest rates and understand the relationship between them.
- Understand the relationship between domestic, international and eurocurrency rates.
- Understand the effect of interest rate changes on the banks, the domestic economy and the balance of payments.

GETTING STARTED

In money-using economies, money creates claims because it is an asset, a store of value, as well as a means of exchange. Therefore those who lend money expect to be recompensed for handing over their claims for the period of the loan to those who borrow money. The recompense is the interest rate. It is expressed as a rate per cent per annum because it is a convenient way of calculating and comparing the cost of borrowing money. Thus one commonly used definition of the interest rate is that it is a 'price' at which money is lent and borrowed.

Borrowers borrow money because they are short of funds to meet their current needs for goods and services, whereas lenders lend funds which are surplus to their current needs for goods and services. Therefore the interest rate can also be defined as the 'price' the lenders expect (and the borrowers pay) for exchanging current claims for greater future claims to goods and services.

MAIN LENDERS AND BORROWERS

In modern economies the principal lenders are often those at one stage removed, since most of their funds are obtained from others.

Individuals lend to banks and other financial institutions by depositing their savings with them, or lend to businesses and the government by directly purchasing their securities and bonds. Bonds are documents with specific repayment dates (except for a few undated bonds), definite rates of interest to be paid and explicit conditions for repayment. Banks on-lend much of their deposits to individuals, firms and countries as overdrafts and term loans. Building societies lend most of their accumulated deposits from the public to house buyers. Finance houses lend funds out of their accumulated borrowings to finance the hire-purchase transactions of the public. Insurance companies collect premiums for various kinds of insurance policies they sell to the public, and then lend or invest significant proportions of their receipts. Firms use their surplus funds to make deposits with banks, or to lend to the government by purchasing government debt, e.g. gilt-edged securities, or lend to other firms against their promises to repay. Governments borrow huge sums of money from anyone who is willing to purchase their securities, and in turn lend a portion of their borrowed funds to nationalized and other industries, to foreign governments and other borrowers. Virtually all of this lending and borrowing activity is linked by the receipt and payment of interest rates.

ESSENTIAL PRINCIPLES
THEORIES OF INTEREST

These theories aim to define 'interest' and to explain why interest is paid.

The productivity theory

According to this theory, interest is paid because capital is productive. Borrowers expect that their productivity will be increased measurably by the use of capital goods (machinery, equipment, premises), and are therefore prepared to pay a part of the increase in productivity to lenders as interest for advancing funds with which to purchase capital goods. The marginal productivity of borrowed capital, i.e. by how much each additional unit borrowed to buy capital goods increases the productivity (and therefore the profits) of the borrower, will determine how high an interest rate the borrower will be willing to pay to the lender. The theory suffers from two chief weaknesses: first, it is a demand side theory because it considers the point of interest payment solely from the borrowers' side, and second, it does not explain the interest payment on non-productive borrowing, e.g. loans to buy consumer goods.

The abstinence theory

This maintains that interest is a reward for saving: saving requires abstinence, i.e. postponing the immediate satisfaction from consumption of one's wealth and income. Saving is postponed spending in order to derive a greater sum than originally saved. The higher the rate of interest offered, the greater the incentive to save. The theory is defective for two main reasons: first, it is solely a supply side theory and completely ignores the idea of productivity to the borrower, and second, it does not explain savings that take place without the inducement of interest, e.g. involuntary savings of the very rich.

The time-preference theory

There are both supply and demand sides to this theory. The quantity and price of funds supplied are determined here by the preferences of those in society for income in the future rather than in the present. The quantity and price of funds demanded are determined by the preferences of those in society who want funds now. The interaction between the supply and demand sides of the preference schedules will determine the equilibrium rate of interest, i.e. the rate of interest acceptable to both sides. The weakness of the theory is that it treats money as merely a neutral means of exchange.

The loanable funds theory

The supply of loanable funds results from savings and the demand for loans arises from investment decisions. According to this theory, the rate of interest is that rate which equates the opportunity cost of savings with the marginal productivity of investment in capital goods. The 'opportunity cost' of savings is the alternative foregone, i.e. the goods that could have been consumed now, had the individual not saved. The loanable funds theory maintains that in a market economy the rate of interest will move up or down to accommodate changes in supply and demand conditions for loanable funds; the suggestion here is that savings and investment decisions are interest-elastic, i.e. sensitive in reaction to interest changes. The theory is defective because it ignores the effects of changes in incomes on interest rates: if incomes increase as a result of an increase in money supply (due to, say, an increase in bank lending and/or public expenditure) the supply of loanable funds will be greater at any rate of interest.

In all the above theories the rate of interest is determined by the volume of savings (supply of loans) or by the marginal productivity of investment (demand for loans) or by interaction between the two. Since both supply and demand are non-monetary considerations in these theories and since money is treated as a passive means of exchange, it is appropriate to class these theories as *non-monetary theories of interest*.

Both savings and productivity considerations are long-term considerations; they do not change overnight. Therefore non-monetary theories are mainly concerned with the long run.

The liquidity preference theory.

This is a monetary theory of interest because it concentrates on the point that money is not merely a neutral means of exchange, but also, and more importantly, a store of value in its own right. According to the theory, individuals and firms make two decisions about their total wealth and income: how much of it to spend and how much of it to save. With the portion they decide to save, they will most probably make the following further decisions:

1. How much of savings to hold in liquid form for day-to-day expenses (*transaction balances*), and to meet some unforeseen

contingency (*precautionary balances*). The total amount of money held in liquid form for these reasons will depend upon:

(a) the level of their incomes and expenditures (the rich will hold more than the poor),

(b) the nature of institutional practices (how frequently they are paid, the availability of overdrafts, the use of credit cards), and

(c) the cost of holding these liquid balances, i.e. the loss of interest involved. Although the demand for transaction and precautionary balances is largely interest-inelastic, it is not absolutely insensitive to the prevailing interest rate: the higher the rate of interest, the greater the incentive to minimize the size of these balances held in liquid, and therefore non- or lower-interest bearing forms.

2. How much of savings to hold in liquid form in order to make capital gains by buying and selling financial assets at the right time (*speculative balances*): buying bonds (sacrificing liquidity) when the interest rate is high, and selling bonds (preferring liquidity) when the interest rate is low. We would expect that the lower the yield (broadly speaking, the interest rate) on securities, the greater the liquidity preference; and the higher the yield, the lower the liquidity preference. In the latter case it costs too much to hold money in non-interest bearing forms when the interest rate is very high. Thus the demand for speculative balances tends to be highly interest-elastic.

The equilibrium rate of interest in liquidity preference theory is that rate which equates the demand to hold money in transaction, precautionary and speculative balances (i.e. the demand for liquidity) with the stock of money (i.e. the supply of liquidity). Thus, according to this theory, the rate of interest is the 'price' which balances the demand for and supply of liquidity, or money.

In the liquidity preference theory, non-monetary considerations of the rate of interest, such as the volume of savings and marginal productivity, play no part in the determination of the rate of interest; the all-important consideration is liquidity preference, i.e. the demand to hold money. It is for this reason that liquidity preference theory is called the monetary theory of interest. Since liquidity preference can change overnight, the chief relevance of this theory is in the short term. Like the loanable funds theory, this theory too ignores the effects of changes in incomes on liquidity preference: the rich hold more money than the poor at any level of interest rates.

USEFUL APPLIED MATERIALS

FACTORS WHICH CAUSE THE INTEREST LEVEL TO CHANGE

There are four main factors: (1) Fluctuations in supply and demand; (2) Rate of inflation; (3) Government intervention; (4) Market expectations.

Fluctuations in the supply of, and demand for, funds	When the economy is on the upswing, trade is brisk, the employment level high and increasing, and the prospects of making profits bright. As a result, the demand for funds, both for investment and consumer goods, tends to be greater than the supply of funds. Consequently, the level of interest rates tends to rise in times of boom, but falls when the economy is moving into recession, although some time lag may be involved.
Rate of inflation	During periods of rapidly rising inflation rate, lenders expect to receive a 'positive' rate of return in order to neutralize the corrosive effect of inflation on their financial assets. The 'nominal' interest rate is a straightforward money rate, e.g. 10 per cent per annum, whereas the 'real' interest rate is the nominal rate adjusted for the *expected* rate of inflation. If the inflation rate is expected to exceed the level of the nominal rate during the period of the loan, the real rate to the lender becomes negative. Therefore, in times of rapidly rising inflation rate, lenders expect a nominal rate which exceeds the expected inflationary rate, in order to earn a positive rate of return on their lending.
Government intervention	A monopolist can either control the supply of his produce or its price, but not both. In like manner, a central bank can control either money supply or interest rates, but not both. If the authorities decide to control the money supply, say, in order to control inflation, then interest rates will take the strain of such a decision; as money supply is reduced, the level of interest rates will rise.
	If government spending is in excess of tax revenues, then, to finance the deficit, the authorities will have to sell government securities fairly quickly. To do this the yield (or interest rate) on securities will be raised sufficiently so that the public is attracted to purchase them quickly. Such activity by the authorities will tend to raise the general level of interest rates; banks and other financial institutions will have to raise their rates to maintain the inflow of funds.
	To counteract excessive downward pressure on the exchange rates of the national currency, caused by the perceived weakness of the currency and/or by higher interest rates in overseas financial centres, the authorities may deliberately raise the level of short-term rates temporarily to attract hoards of interest-sensitive 'hot' money balances.
Market expectations	If the market expectations are that the authorities are succeeding in their counter-inflationary policies, and that a relaxed monetary control policy is in the offing, then such market expectations will help bring about a fall in interest rates. For instance, lenders will no longer seek such a high nominal interest rate to cushion them against future inflation.
THE WAY IN WHICH THE BANK OF ENGLAND FIXES SHORT-TERM RATES	The Bank of England, as the Central Bank of the UK, has aimed to keep the *very short-term* (up to one month) interest rates within a narrow unpublished band, but to allow market forces in the money markets a greater role in determining the *longer-term* rates. This policy helps shape the structure of money market rates.

The control of the Bank over the very short-term rates is assured, for two main reasons.

1. It offsets, at its own terms, shortages (or surpluses) of cash in the money markets via the discount houses; in this way, it can control the marginal cost of funds to the banking system. In theory, the Bank is not expected to act as the lender of last resort to the banking system, yet in practice it does; it has to, for it cannot abdicate its responsibilities as the central bank!

2. In its money market operations, the Bank buys and sells eligible commercial bills and Treasury bills in the discount market in four bands, according to the maturity of the bills. The bands where the Bank's control is the strongest are bands one and two, i.e. bands in which bills have maturities of up to 14 days and one month respectively. Bands three and four include bills with longer maturities; in these bands the Bank's direct influence is less strong. Changes in the Bank's dealing rate in bands one and two are taken by the money markets to mean that the Bank intends to bring about a change in the cost of marginal funds and therefore in the general level of short-term money market rates. Clearly if the Bank makes short-term funds more expensive to the banking system, the banks in turn will charge more for overdrafts and short-term loans. Thus despite the suspension (not abolition) of the Minimum Lending Rate in August 1981, the Bank exerts the key influence on the level of short-term rates in the money markets. The interaction between the bill operations of the Bank and market expectations is the main determinant of the level and structure of short-term rates in the UK, and it plays an important part in determining long-term rates in the money markets.

With the more aggressive deposit-gathering stance of the building societies, the clearers have come to rely increasingly on funds from the money markets e.g. wholesale deposits – in recent years. Still more recently, clearers have themselves been collecting higher interest-bearing retail deposits. Therefore, bank base rates will have broadly to move in line with the money market rates. In fact, after December 1973, the clearers even geared the advances made to certain customers to market rates rather than to base rates. Using market rates such as the sterling London Inter-Bank Offered Rate (LIBOR) as the basis for setting interest rates on term lending is of benefit to the banks; it gives them the opportunity to match their lending rates and conditions with those for the wholesale deposits they obtain through the inter-bank market. Non-bank financial institutions who, like banks, obtain wholesale funds, apply a similar criterion in on-lending for longer-terms. Thus, although the Bank only openly fixes the short-term rates, yet the direction given by it to short-term rates permeates right through the whole spectrum of interest rates in the monetary system.

THE EFFECTS OF CHANGES IN THE GENERAL LEVEL OF INTEREST RATES ON BANKS

1. The effects of a *fall* in interest rates

(a) It will reduce both the cost of funds acquired by banks and the interest received by them from advances. However, if the demand for advances is interest-elastic, the total advances might rise substantially; increased advances will create increased deposits in the banking system as a whole and may improve the banks' profitability.

(b) It will squeeze the net return or the 'endowment' effect of the non-interest bearing accounts of the retail banks considerably, thus reducing their profitability. On the other hand, their profit margins on fixed-rate lending would be increased.

(c) Building societies have been slow to reduce their interest rates on deposits; *banks* have been relatively quicker to reduce their deposit rates as the level of interest rates falls, and have therefore tended to lose retail deposits to building societies as interest rates fall.

(d) Banks, in order to maintain acceptable profitability levels, might widen the margin between interest paid and interest received, and might also increase service and commission charges.

(e) A fall in interest rates would increase the capital value of the banks' fixed interest investments; banks might realize the capital gains by selling some of these investments.

(f) The loan repayments burden of banks' customers is reduced when interest rates fall; therefore there will be fewer bad debts and the banks would probably reduce their bad debt provisions.

(g) To ward off the adverse effect of falls in interest rates, banking groups may actively encourage lending at fixed rates via their subsidiaries, e.g. hire purchase companies.

2. The effects of a *rise* in interest rates

By and large, the effects on banks of a rise in interest rates would be exactly opposite to those of a fall in interest rates.

(a) Higher loan and deposit rates of the banks might suggest that their profit margins would remain unchanged, but for retail banks margins improve because of the endowment effect of non-interest bearing deposits. On the other hand, their profit margins are reduced on fixed-rate lending.

(b) Higher price of loans may reduce loan demand of the banks' business customers; although in practice necessity overcomes price, at least in the short term. The demand for loans for capital goods, and more particularly working capital, tends to be interest-inelastic, and therefore, provided that profit margins are maintained, the loan demand for capital goods by the banks' private sector business customers is unlikely to change. The same is true of public sector investment expenditure.

(c) Banks are in competition with non-bank financial institutions, chiefly building societies, National Savings and the government, for the savings and deposits of the public. Whether the banks' deposit inflow would increase or decrease would largely depend upon how well the banks' interest rate structure compared with that of the other financial institutions and with that offered on government securities. Apart from the banks' large sophisticated corporate depositors, most of the other depositors tend to be sluggish in switching their deposits between financial institutions.

(d) High interest rates tend to depress the economy by depressing demand in certain sectors of the economy, e.g. in the consumer goods industry. The more the economy becomes depressed, the lower are profits and the greater becomes the significance of the interest rate bills for business firms; this may lead to more bad debts for the banks, who would probably have to increase their bad debt provisions.

(e) Higher interest rates in the UK would tend to act as a magnet for large hot money balances and this would raise the exchange rate of the pound. The rise in the exchange rate would reduce the value, in sterling, of overseas residents' deposits and of the earnings of the overseas subsidiaries of the UK parent banks, thus reducing their profitability. A higher exchange rate would also reduce the competitiveness of UK exports and import substitutes, tending further to depress the economy as in (d) above.

BANKS' BASE RATES

The clearing and other deposit-taking commercial banks cater for the major proportion of the borrowing needs of the public, other than house purchase. Although the rates payable by customers are a matter for negotiation, most lending banks quote a 'base rate' and grant overdrafts at a fixed margin over this rate. Until the competition and credit control measures were implemented in 1971, the UK banks, especially the clearers, had a collective policy on interest rates, i.e. their rates moved up or down in concert. However, since 1971, the banks have agreed to abandon their collective policy on interest rates, and each bank establishes its own base rate and deposit rate. It was expected that this would create competition among banks, which would bring down interest rates to the benefit of general borrowers. For a few months, there was obvious competition and the rates did come down. Banks still do compete with each other, but since most large borrowers tend to be interest-rate sensitive, it is unusual for there to be a significant difference in base rates for any length of time; competition is therefore unlikely to lead to the level of rates coming down, although, of course, it has led to a reduction in margins over base rate.

An extreme influence on bank base rates concerns arbitrage. *Arbitrage* occurs when market rates, generally inter-bank rates, which vary daily in response to supply and demand for funds, are higher than base rates, which do not change quite as often. Then the banks' big customers can borrow from the banks at base rate plus one (blue chip rate), and re-lend the borrowed funds in the money markets at a profit; this process is called '*hard arbitrage*' or '*round tripping*'. '*Soft arbitrage'* occurs when the banks' large customers pay off their overdrafts by borrowing from the money markets at interest rates lower than the base rate plus one. Arbitrage of either sort has led to the growth in LIBOR-linked lending, because such lending can never lead to arbitrage. It has also led to base rates changing much more quickly than was once the case.

THE PATTERN OF INTEREST RATES

Although many of the interest theories assume that there is **one** rate of interest, which moves up or down, this is, in reality, both incorrect and misleading. You have only to look at the daily, and especially the Sunday, newspapers to notice the wide pattern of interest rates. For example, the sterling money rates prevailing in London are shown overleaf in Table 2.

The two most important sets of rates are those under 'Interbank' and 'Eligible bank bills'. The double-barrelled quotation of rates displays the spread between the bid (deposit) and offered (lending) rates. Where there is a single rate, it is the offered rate.

The existence of so many interest rates broadly reflects variations in the risk, supply and demand considerations and period of loans. Lenders are willing to accept lower interest rates from those borrowers who minimize lending risks.

The lending risks

The *lending risks* may take the following forms:

1. The risk of default

The borrower may become unable to repay the loan. For this reason, for three-month money, Treasury bills (government IOUs) are considered safer by lenders than, say, bank deposits; therefore Treasury bills offer a slightly lower rate of return than do bank deposits. Similarly, banks offer a slightly lower interest on savings deposits than do building societies or finance houses.

2. The loss of liquidity

That is, how quickly, conveniently, and without significant loss in income and/or capital value the lender can convert his lending (e.g. bond, share certificate) into cash. The greater the loss of liquidity, the higher normally will be the rate of return. For example, banks offer a higher rate on *term deposits* than on *seven-day deposits*, and building societies offer higher returns on *deposits* which have a *penalty clause* for immediate withdrawals, than for *normal share deposits*. The concern with the liquidity aspect of lending is reflected in the preference of lenders for relatively short-term lending. However, money is borrowed, especially by business firms, for relatively long periods of time. Consequently there is a greater supply of short-term funds, but a greater demand for long-term borrowing; hence, short-term lending usually earns a lower rate of interest, and borrowers wanting longer-term loans have to offer higher rates to overcome the lenders' reluctance to part with liquidity for longer periods.

3. *Fall in market value*

The market value of the asset held by the lender may fall. A major reason for this lending risk, especially for fixed-interest lending, is rapidly rising inflation. In times of a rising inflation rate, the longer the maturity period of a loan, the greater the lending risk. Therefore in such times lenders expect to receive a rate of interest which is higher than the *expected* rate of inflation; or alternatively that their lending should be index-linked; index-linked securities yield positive, real rates.

4. *Capital loss considerations*

Suppose that the general level of interest rates is 10 per cent per annum, but that it is expected to rise. An investor buying a £100 bond with a 10 per cent per annum yield will expect to receive £10 every year until the bond matures for repayment. Suppose, later on, that the general level of interest rates rises to 20 per cent per annum; this will cause the *market price* of the 10 per cent per annum bond to fall to £50: an investor wanting a £10 per annum return will only have to pay £50 for a new bond yielding 20 per cent per annum. An expected (or actual) rise in interest rates means a fall in the market price of fixed-interest lending, i.e. a capital loss or depreciation; conversely, an expected (or actual) fall in interest rates will cause the market price of fixed-interest lending to rise, i.e. it will benefit from a capital gain or appreciation. Therefore if investors expect interest rates to rise in the future, they will require higher rates than currently available to compensate for the probable capital loss.

Lenders may however be willing to accept a lower rate of interest for longer-term lending if they strongly expect a substantial **fall** in the general level of interest rates, in the hope of making a gain on the capital value of their lending.

Table 2

October 11	Sterling CDs	Interbank	Local auth. deposits	Finance house deposits
Overnight	—	2–10¾	11½	—
Seven-day notice	—	11¼–11 13/16	11½	—
One month	11⅝–11 11/16	11⅝–11¾	11 11/16	11⅝
Three months	11 5/16–11 7/16	—	11½	11 17/32
Six months	11–11⅛	—	11 3/16	11¼
One year	10 3/16–10 15/16	—	11 1/16	11⅛

London Clearing Banks Base Rate: 11½ per cent (since July 30)

Note how rates vary, both between markets and over different time periods.

Source: *Financial Times*, 14 October 1985.

THE TERM STRUCTURE OF INTEREST RATES

This means the level of short- and long-term rates and the relationship between them. This relationship can be seen in the movements of the normal money market curve, viz. the *yield curve* (Fig. 1). A yield curve is the relationship between yields on similar financial assets with different terms to maturity. Its steepness shows that generally the **longer** the term to maturity, the **higher the yield, because lenders require a larger compensation for a more sustained loss of liquidity, a higher lending risk and greater uncertainty.**

Curve 1 is the normal money market yield curve which slopes upwards signifying that, other things being equal, lenders lending for longer terms require larger compensation for loss of liquidity, higher lending risks and greater uncertainty. They are not expecting any future interest rate changes.

The 'other things being equal' assumption is upset, chiefly, by the role of *expectations*. If the expectation of the majority of lenders is that the future rates will *fall*, then long rates will be below short rates, as shown by the yield *curve 2*; here the long rates will tend to approximate to the *average* of expected future rates.

Suppose the current market rate is 11 per cent per annum, but is expected to fall over the year as follows: after three months to 10.5 per cent p.a., after six months to 10 per cent p.a. and after nine months to 9.5 per cent p.a. A bank makes a loan of £500,000 to a business customer for one year. What rate should the bank charge to the customer, taking into account the expected fall in rates over the

Company deposits	Discount market deposits	Treasury bills	Eligible bank bills	Fine trade bills
8–11⅝	1½–11½	—	—	—
11¾–11⅞	11⅝–11¾	—	—	—
11⅞	11¼	11¹¹/₃₂	11¹¹/₃₂	11³¹/₃₂
11¾	11	11⅛	11³/₃₂	11²³/₃₂
—	11	—	10¹⁹/₃₂	11⁷/₃₂
—	—	—	—	—

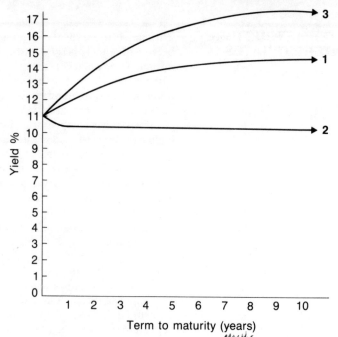

Fig. 1. Yield curves

Months.

year? The following schedule shows the bank's interest earnings for each quarter, during the year (compound interest considerations which would be relevant in an actual case of this kind, are ignored, to keep the calculations straightforward).

Interest earned for the first 3 months
$$= \frac{£500,000 \times 0.25 \times 11}{100} = £13,750$$

Interest earned for the second 3 months
$$= \frac{£500,000 \times 0.25 \times 10.5}{100} = £13,125$$

Interest earned for the third 3 months
$$= \frac{£500,000 \times 0.25 \times 10}{100} = £12,500$$

Interest earned for the fourth 3 months
$$= \frac{£500,000 \times 0.25 \times 9.5}{100} = £11,875$$

Total interest earned for the whole year $= £51,250$

The average of the four short-term rates
$$= \frac{11 + 10.5 + 10 + 9.5}{4} = 10.25 \text{ per cent.}$$

The bank will charge a rate of 10.25 per cent to the customer. Thus, although the current short rate (three months) is 11 per cent per annum, the longer rate (one year) is lower at 10.25 per cent per annum; this is because future interest rates are expected to fall over the year. If, after one year, future interest rates are expected to stabilize at 10.25 per cent, then the yield curve will become horizontal at 10.25 per cent, as in yield curve 2.

If current short rates are higher than long rates, this could be due to several reasons:

1. Future interest rates are expected to fall.
2. The high short rates are expected to be temporary; perhaps the need of banks and other financial institutions for funds to balance their books at the end of each financial year and half-year has pushed short rates up temporarily.
3. The monetary authorities have raised short-term rates in response to general economic developments; for example, to deal with a downward pressure on the exchange rate, the authorities may deliberately raise short-term rates temporarily, in order to encourage the inflow of 'hot' money balances and to discourage the outflow of funds.
4. The belief that the authorities will succeed in curbing inflation soon, hence the expectation that a relaxed monetary policy, with lower interest rates, will follow.

Yield *Curve 3* reflects a situation in which the expectation of the majority of lenders is that interest rates will rise, and therefore that the capital value of lending will fall; hence long rates will be much higher than short rates.

To maximize the returns from lending, lenders will, other things being equal, switch between longer and shorter loans/bonds according to their expected yields over the period for which they wish to lend. There is no further gain to be made by such switching when the yield on long loans is equal to the average of the expected yields on short loans during the period in question (as shown by the above calculations). If lenders then begin to expect a rise in future rates, they would prefer to lend short-term so that on maturity they may lend the repayments at higher rates. Conversely, if they begin to expect future rates to fall, they would prefer to lend long at fixed rates in order to make capital gains as the level of interest rates falls.

While the short-term interest rates in the UK rose sharply in January 1985 (to 14 per cent), longer term rates increased much less. As a result the yield curve has been downward sloping for most of 1985, reflecting the expectation that short-term rates would not stay high for too long.

RECENT EXAMINATION QUESTIONS

The following six questions give an indiction of the types of questions you will need to answer on interest rates. You could usefully spend ten minutes or so on each question, trying to identify the main points you would use in your answer, before turning to the outline answers below.

Question 1.	What do you understand by the term 'yield curve'? Discuss the factors which influence the relationship between short-term and long-term interest rates. Illustrate your answer by reference to recent experience in the United Kingdom or any other country with which you are familiar.
Question 2.	To what extent does the Bank of England now attempt to influence the general level of interest rates? Include in your answer an analysis of the Bank of England's operations in the money markets.
Question 3.	Discuss the factors which affect the level and pattern of money market interest rates in the United Kingdom. To what extent do changes in money market rates lead to changes in commercial banks' base rates?
Question 4.	Distinguish between nominal and real rates of interest. For what reasons might a country experience: (a) a high level of nominal interest rates; (b) high real rates of interest?
Question 5.	What do you understand by the 'term structure' of interest rates? Explain in detail the factors which influence the relationship between short-term and long-term interest rates.
Question 6.	Why, in practice, are there so many different rates of interest in a country such as the UK?

OUTLINE ANSWERS

Answer 1

(a) Yield curve is the relationship between yields on similar financial assets with different terms to maturity (Fig. 1).
(b) Factors which influence short- and long-term interest rates:
- Liquidity preference: higher compensation (interest rates) for lenders lending long.
- Lending risks: higher rates for lending long because risks are higher in long loans (since yields on *similar* assets is being considered, discussion of the different types of borrowers would be inappropriate).
- Role of expectations: long rates should approximate to the average of expected short rates.
(c) In the UK short rates have often been higher than long rates because:
- high short rates expected to be temporary;
- expectation that the rising inflation rate has been controlled.

Answer 2.

MLR suspended in 1981; since then no *direct* control by the Bank of England of the level of short rates and the banks' base rates.
- Via its money market operations, the Bank aims to keep the very short-term (up to 14 days) rates within an 'unpublished' band while allowing market forces greater influence in determining the structure of longer rates.

- The terms of the 'last resort' finance to the banking system, which the Bank still provides, determine the marginal cost of funds to the banking system; this affects the banks' base rates.
- The last resort finance is provided, almost exclusively, via the discount houses, through the purchase and sale of commercial bills at the Bank's terms: changes in these terms invariably cause changes in the banks' base rates.
- Although the Bank does not aim to control longer-term rates, yet the changes caused in very short rates by alterations in the terms of its bill dealings, *indirectly* influence longer rates as well.

Answer 3.

Two-part question; make sure you answer both parts.

1. (a) Determination of short rates:
      Bank of England exerts the major influence:
      - controls marginal cost of funds to the banking system through its operations in the bill markets, via discount houses.
      - Interaction between the Bank's bill operations and money market expectations is the chief determinant.
   (b) Long rates greatly influenced by the above two points.

2. Bank base rates depend upon:
   - wholesale rates in the inter-bank market (LIBOR), because of less dependence on traditional retail deposits and more on wholesale funds. Base rates move in line with short-term (up to three months) money market rates.
   - the extent of competition for deposits.
   - the monetary policy directives.
   - the rate of inflation – positive returns.
   - the rates in overseas financial centres.

Answer 4.

Nominal rates are the actual rates charged or paid.

- Real rates are nominal rates adjusted for the *expected* rate of inflation: the longer the period of a loan, the greater the difficulty of assessing the appropriate adjustment allowance.
- High nominal rates reflect:
  (i) high rate of inflation;
  (ii) official high interest rate policy to control inflation;
  (iii) higher interest rates overseas.
- High real rates result from:
  (i) official interest rate policy pushing up nominal rates above the rate of inflation to create positive real rates for lenders and borrowers;
  (ii) budget deficits in countries with strong economies;
  (iii) loanable funds theory: in a market economy, the rate of interest will move up or down to accommodate changes in the supply (propensity to save) and demand (marginal productivity of capital) conditions of loanable funds.

Answer 5.

'Term structure' means the way in which the yield on a financial asset varies according to the length of the borrowing: a yield curve diagram illustrates the term structure.

- The longer the term, other things being equal, the higher the rate expected on the *same* or similar assets.
- Factors influencing the relationship between short-term and long-term interest rates:
  (i)   long rates higher than short rates to compensate for longer loss of liquidity and greater risk;
  (ii) expectations of future movements in interest rates.

Answer 6.

Reasons for so many interest rates:

- Risk element: e.g. Treasury bills considered safer than bank deposits, therefore offer lower rate of return; the rate may become even lower if Treasury bills are in short supply.
- Time element – yield curve explanation.
- Size of loan: larger loans may attract higher rates.
- Cost of funds in the wholesale money markets.
- Type of currency involved, e.g. eurocurrency rates generally lower than sterling rates.
- Consumer Credit Act requires the publication of the true rate as well as the flat rate for personal loans.
- Floating base rates: to estimate the future course of interest rates, for term loans, to crystallize customer's repayments.
- Bank of England's bill dealing rate: determined administratively, not by the market.
- Status of the borrower, e.g. blue chip rate (base rate + 1) for blue chip customers only.

A TUTOR'S ANSWER

A specimen answer is given below to a question on Interest Rates, on an aspect of interest rates which is of increasing importance. The answer plan is intended to help you assess the scope of the question. Try to plan an answer to the question yourself before turning to the answer plan given below, and the full specimen answer.

Question

Assess the likely effects of an increase in the general level of interest rates on:
(a) a country's economy;
(b) the commercial banks.

Answer plan
Effects of an *increase* only to be discussed.
(a) (i)   deflationary effects;
    (ii) inflationary effects;
    (iii) balance of payments effects.
(b) (i)   effects on profit margins;
    (ii) endowment effect;

Specimen answer

Higher interest rates will tend to depress demand, output and employment levels because all these are to some degree sensitive to changes in interest rates.

Consumer spending is likely to be reduced for three main reasons: higher cost of consumer credit, higher mortgage payments and higher prices of consumer goods (assuming the consumer goods industry passes its own higher costs on to the consumers). The demand for consumer goods, due to more expensive loans and higher prices, will tend to decrease, which in turn will cause contraction of output and employment within the consumer goods industry. The increase in unemployment will reduce tax revenue and increase government spending, particularly on unemployment benefits.

The effect on the capital goods industry will be different, largely because the demand for capital goods tends to be interest-inelastic. Since a large part of capital expenditure comes from the public sector, and public sector expenditure of this type is highly insensitive to interest rate changes, capital expenditure will therefore be little affected by higher interest rates. Output and employment within the capital goods industry will, provided profit margins are maintained, remain largely unchanged by higher interest rates.

Higher interest rates will tend to attract short-term investment and speculative balances from overseas to take advantage of any interest rate differential. Assuming that the conversion of hot money balances into the national currency is on a large scale, it will increase the exchange rate of the national currency. The higher exchange rate will raise export prices, making exports less competitive, and reduce import prices, making imports more attractive. If the elasticities of demand for exports abroad and for imports internally are sufficiently elastic, then not only will the balance of payments go into deficit, but domestic output and employment will also be reduced by the production of fewer exports and by the increased penetration of imports.

Higher interest rates will also increase the cost of export finance which, in turn, will increase export costs and, possibly, export prices. However, this *direct* effect of higher interest rates on exports is likely to be less significant – interest costs are a small part of the selling price of exports – than the *indirect* effect of the higher exchange rate.

Higher interest rates, at least in the short term, will tend to increase the level of inflation, because of higher industrial costs of production and higher mortgage costs. On the other hand, higher interest rates will have a deflationary effect on aggregate demand, cutting consumption, investment and exports. This will 'weaken' both goods and labour markets, which would mean reduced profit margins and lower pay settlements, i.e. lower inflation. Cheaper imports, because of the high exchange rate, and a reduced money supply, because of high interest rates, may again lead to lower inflation.

A general statement that higher interest rates increase bank profits is incorrect. The banking system may be divided into wholesale banking and retail banking. *Wholesale banking* (e.g. merchant banks) will not be much influenced by an increase in interest rates, because it relies to a much greater extent on the *margins* between lending and borrowing rates for its profits, rather than on actual rates. Higher loan *and* deposit rates for the wholesale banks would mean that their profit margins would largely remain unchanged.

For *retail banks* (e.g. clearing banks), higher loan rates also mean higher deposit rates, and therefore the increase in the profitability due to higher lending rates is largely offset by higher deposit rates. However, the profit margins of retail banks increase from the 'endowment effect' of their non-interest bearing deposits, i.e. the increase in net returns on non-interest bearing current accounts. On the other hand, their profit margins would be reduced on fixed-rate lending. Also, due to a fall in the value of assets charged as security for bank advances, their capital value may fall as interest rates rise. Furthermore, the authorities may claw back a portion of the extra profit from the endowment effect by imposing a windfall tax. This may explain, in part, why some banks traditionally choose to reduce the margins between deposit and lending rates when interest rates are rising, and to increase them when interest rates are falling.

There will be several likely changes on a bank's balance sheet from an increase in interest rates. The higher price of loans may reduce loan demand to buy consumer goods, if not capital goods. However, 'distress borrowing', especially by businessmen, is interest-inelastic and will still take place, increasing the retail banks' profitability. An increase in interest rates results in higher interest rate bills for bank customers, especially large borrowers; this may cause an increase in the bad debt rate and the banks would have to increase their bad debt provisions, which will reduce profitability. The effect on banks' deposit-taking vis-à-vis their competitors, especially building societies, would largely depend upon how well the interest rate structure of banks compares with that of their competitors. Building societies, unlike banks, have been slow to change their rates in response to changes in market rates, and it is likely that the banks' inflow of deposits may increase temporarily at the expense of building societies. Against this, an increase in interest rates slows down the growth of current accounts, since the opportunity cost of holding such accounts is more interest foregone. If interest rates are expected to fall in the future, fixed-interest government securities become more attractive, which may further curtail the banks' current accounts.

A STEP FURTHER

Interest rates are an item of vital concern to banks. The *Financial Times* is an invaluable source of up-to-date data and information on the level, structure and pattern of interest rates. There are also many useful articles on interest rates and interest rate-related issues in the past editions of the *Financial Times*, which can be located via the *Financial Times Monthly Index*. The *Examiners' Reports* and *Updating Notes* published by The Institute of Bankers highlight those areas of interest rates which are most important to bankers. Articles in the quality financial press and in banking magazines will keep you abreast of major changes in this topic of the syllabus.

Chapter 7

Balance of payments

- Appreciate the importance of the balance of payments.
- Understand the structure of the balance of payments accounts – the balance of trade, the balance of payments, currency flows and official financing.
- Analyse the causes of changes in the terms of trade and of their relationship to the balance of trade and the balance of payments.
- Understand the methods of both financing and correcting a surplus or deficit in the balance of payments, including the principles and practice of protectionism.

GETTING STARTED

A country imports those goods and services which it needs but is either unable to produce internally, or which it can only produce at uncompetitive cost or inferior quality. It pays for the imports of such goods and services largely by its foreign currency earnings from exports. The balance of payments of any country records the revenues and payments from all economic transactions between its government, firms (including their foreign subsidiaries) and residents, and the governments, firms and residents of those countries with which it trades. The balance of payments is an account and, like any other account, it must balance.

The importance of the balance of payments position to a country is that if it has exported more goods and services than it has imported, then it is a creditor country and stands to receive payments in foreign currencies. These can be used to build up its currency reserves, or to repay any loans, or to invest overseas. Conversely, if it has imported more goods and services than it has exported over a period of time, then it is a debtor country, and has to make good the deficit by drawing on its currency reserves or by borrowing overseas or by selling its valuable assets and foreign investments. A chronic balance of payments deficit for a country suggests to the rest of the world that it is unable to pay its way in international trade and investment, which reflects badly on its government, firms and citizens.

A country's foreign currency and gold reserves are finite and its ability to borrow overseas or raise funds in some other ways is not without limit. Therefore, a country with a continuous balance of payments deficit runs the distinct risk of being treated as a bad debtor by its trading partners, who may refuse to sell it the goods and services it needs. If this happens, then its economic growth will be badly hit and the level of employment and the standard of living of its residents will fall significantly.

It is therefore of utmost importance for the government of a country suffering from a prolonged deficit on its external account to take such measures internally as will encourage its exports and discourage its imports, so that the deficit on its balance of payments is rectified and it is once again able to pay its way in the world.

ESSENTIAL PRINCIPLES

TERMS OF TRADE

Over a period of time, the terms of trade compare changes in the prices of a country's exports with changes in the prices of its imports. The changes in export prices are expressed as a percentage of changes in import prices, and then presented as an index, with some base year as 100. The terms of trade index of a country is determined by the following formula:

$$\frac{\text{Average price of exports}}{\text{Average price of imports}} \times 100$$

If the index increases, compared to a base year of 100, the terms of trade are said to have 'improved', i.e. a given quantity of exports will purchase more imports than before. Thus, if the index of export prices of a country has risen over a period of years from 100 to 119, and its index of import prices has fallen over the same period of years from 100 to 97, then the terms of trade of the country are said to have improved over the period by the ratio 119/97 × 100 = 122.68 per cent. If the terms of trade index in the base year was 100, then, in the above example, the purchasing power of a fixed bundle of exports rose over the period by 22.68 per cent, i.e. 22.68 per cent more imports could be purchased at the end of the period than were purchased by the same fixed quantity of exports in the base year. Note that the terms of trade refer to the multilateral trade of a country and not to its bilateral trade.

Changes in the terms of trade, i.e. changes in the prices of exports and imports, affect the *values* of exports and imports. Since values are quantities multiplied by prices, the relative elasticities of demand for exports and imports will be vital in determining whether the total receipts from exports or the total payments for imports will rise or fall as export and import prices change. If the overseas demand for a country's *exports is elastic* then, other things being equal, its total receipts from exports will be greater at *lower* export prices, i.e. when the terms of trade have 'deteriorated'. If the overseas demand for its *exports is inelastic*, then total receipts from exports will be greater at *higher* export prices, i.e. when the terms of trade have 'improved'. Similarly, if the domestic demand for its *imports is elastic* then, other things being equal, its import bill will be greater at *lower* import prices, i.e. when the terms of trade have 'improved'; if the demand for its *imports is inelastic*, its import bill will be greater at *higher* import prices, i.e. when the terms of trade have 'deteriorated'. Clearly the terms 'improvement' and 'deterioration' must be treated with caution when applied to the terms of trade.

There are gains to be made by countries specializing in the commodities they are relatively most efficient in producing, and exporting the surpluses for imports. However, if the terms of trade deteriorate, then the *exchange* advantage will be less than before. This does not mean however that the gains from trade will necessarily grow just because the terms of trade 'improve'. For instance, a rise in the price of exports may – unless demand for exports is inelastic – be associated with a fall in the *volume* of exports. Any cut in the volume of trade will clearly diminish the gains from specialization and trade.

Changes in the prices of exports and imports result from various factors affecting the conditions of supply and demand for goods which are traded on international markets. *Producers* of a good for which there is a worldwide inelastic demand may exploit their *monopoly* position and raise the price of the product several times over, thereby improving their terms of trade. On the other hand, the major *buyers* of certain products may exploit their *monopsony* position by deliberately witholding demand, thereby causing the terms of trade of the suppliers of such products to deteriorate.

Shortages of food and raw materials in industrialized countries, or increases in demand for such commodities via higher real incomes or population growth, will tend to improve the terms of trade of *primary goods-producing* countries. On the other hand, technical progress may cause the terms of trade of primary goods-producing countries to deteriorate; for instance if the new information technologies economize on the need for raw materials in production.

STRUCTURE OF BALANCE OF PAYMENTS ACCOUNTS	There are five components of the balance of payments account: (1) Current account: (2) Capital account: (3) Total currency flow: (4) Balancing item: (5) Official financing.
Current account	There are two sections in this account: (a) The visible trade balance (or balance of trade). An excess of exports of goods over imports of goods results in a surplus balance of trade ($+$); an excess of imports of goods over exports of goods results in a deficit balance of trade ($-$). A surplus on

visible trade means, other things being equal, an inflow of foreign currency; a deficit means an outflow of foreign currency.

(b) *The Invisible trade balance*. The 'invisible' earnings of a country result from the sale of services (banking, shipping, insurance; tourism and other financial services); the receipt of transfer payments (e.g. receipts by residents of monies transferred by relatives abroad, and more recently payments to the EEC and refunds from them); the receipt of interest (payments from abroad for investments held abroad); and the receipt of profits (from successful trading by overseas subsidiaries) and dividends (from the ownership of the share capital of foreign firms and their subsidiaries). The 'invisible' payments are in respect of the above items, but in reverse.

A surplus (+) on the 'invisible' trade balance suggests an excess of 'invisible' receipts over 'invisible' payments, and a deficit (−) on the 'invisible' trade balance suggests an excess of 'invisible' payments over 'invisible' receipts. As with the visible trade balance, a '+' or a '−' on the invisible balance will, other things being equal, result in an inflow or outflow respectively of foreign currency.

The *current account* is the sum of the visible and invisible trade balances.

Capital account

Capital transactions include *official* capital transactions (government and governmental agencies) and *private* capital transactions (long-term and short-term, direct and indirect, investment and speculative balances).

Private long-term balances are attracted overseas by the prospect of greater profits on investments; private short-term funds (hot money) are attracted overseas by the prospect of short-term gains, either because of interest rates differentials, or because of the possibility of exchange rate movements in the leading international financial centres. In addition to the above capital transactions, there are borrowings and lendings by banks and other financial institutions, and import and export credits, i.e. importers delaying payments or exporters allowing delayed payments. The net balance (±) on the capital account denotes the excess of inflow or of outflow of investment and other capital currency flows for a country.

Total currency flow

When the net (±) balance on the current account is added to the net (±) balance on the capital account, the result is the *total currency flow* (±); this is the total currency that a country stands to receive, or has to pay, as a result of all its transactions with the rest of the world. Sometimes the total currency flow is called the balance of payments.

Balancing item

This balances the difference between the *actual* amount of currency received by the monetary authorities of a country and the amount that they *should* have received as recorded in the current and capital accounts. The imbalance between what has been received, and what should have been received results from errors and omissions in the recording of payments. If the balancing item is positive (+), then *more* foreign currency has actually been received than the recorded items show; if it is negative ($-$), then less foreign money has actually been received than the recorded items show. Over a number of years, $+$ and $-$ values for errors and omissions largely tend to cancel each other out.

Official financing	When the current account, capital account and the balancing item have been added together, the resultant balance is known as the Balance for Official Financing (BOF). The value of BOF ($\pm$) shows the value of the total inflow ($+$) or the total outflow ($-$) of foreign currency during a given period of time. The function of official financing is to balance the balance of payments account, and it shows how a surplus is used and how a deficit is financed. If, for instance, there is a positive ($+$) balance for official financing, then the authorities will utilize this surplus in building up foreign currency reserves, in paying past currency debts, and in investing or lending abroad. On the other hand, if the balance for official financing is negative ($-$), the authorities may finance it by borrowing currency from the central banks of surplus countries, from the IMF or from eurocurrency markets. Another method of official financing is to reduce official gold and foreign currency reserves of the country. Note that 'financing' a balance of payments deficit or surplus is different from 'rectifying' a balance of payments deficit or surplus. Table 3 (pp. 117–118) provides an outline of the main headings and sub-headings of the UK balance of payments accounts.
PROTECTIONISM AND OTHER DIRECT CONTROLS	In order to protect home industries and employment against foreign competition and to become self-sufficient in essential goods, a country may seek to protect itself against imports. Import barriers may take any of the following forms:
Import tariffs	When home products and foreign substitutes are equally priced, an import duty which is higher than any domestic excise duty is protective; it raises the price of foreign substitutes above the price of the domestic product, making home products more attractive.
Subsidies	The government gives direct grants to home producers to reduce their unit costs and give them a price advantage over imported goods.
Export premiums	Exporters are given rebates or refunds of taxation on exports to encourage the expansion of existing industries.
Quotas	A specified volume or value of imports is allowed during a given period.
Exchange control	The central bank does not release foreign currency to pay for imports, or only releases it at a premium or against import licences.
Physical controls	A complete embargo may be imposed on imports from certain countries. Of the above protective methods, only import tariffs provide

income for the government practising protection. In the UK, protection in one form or another has been practised since 1932. Protective measures are often 'hidden', in the form of credit guarantees, cheaper finance to exporters, import deposits and excessive documentation against imports.

Most trading countries accept that an international trade free from protection will benefit all participants. To free international trade from trade barriers, associations such as the General Agreement on Tariffs and Trade (GATT) have been set up. Although GATT, with over 100 member countries, has succeeded in reducing import tariffs to an appreciable extent, the aim of complete free trade among members still remains an ideal.

ADJUSTING IMBALANCES IN THE BALANCE OF PAYMENTS

As we have already noted, no country can continue to have a balance of payments deficit year after year. However, no country may continue to have a balance of payments *surplus*, for at least two reasons.

1. It means that such a country is continuously selling more to the rest of the world, and buying less from it. This is likely to mean that the export earnings of *other countries* in the surplus country's currency are less than is required; therefore they will become less and less able to buy and pay for the surplus country's exports. It may even be in the surplus country's own interest to work off its surplus by increasing its imports from the rest of the world.
2. If the surplus country refuses to increase imports, it may lead other countries to erect trade barriers against its exports via prohibitive import duties, stringent import quotas or even an embargo on its exports.

ADJUSTING A BALANCE OF PAYMENTS SURPLUS

Under freely floating exchange rates, the adjustment should be automatic via the market mechanism. The demand for the surplus country's currency will be high, because the rest of the world will need its currency to pay for their imports; this will push up the exchange rate of the surplus country's currency, making its exports expensive and its imports cheaper and more attractive. The higher exchange rate will, other things being equal, tend to eliminate the surplus and bring about an automatic equilibrium in its balance of payments. If 'other things' are not equal, e.g. there is inelastic demand for its exports, then the government of the surplus country will need to take deliberate policy action to discourage exports and the inflow of capital, and to encourage imports and the outflow of capital.

The following are possible policy measures which the government may take to correct a *surplus* on its balance of payments on current account.

Expansion of home demand

This may be achieved by reducing taxes, lowering interest rates, lifting credit restraints and increasing public expenditure. The increase in home demand would divert export production to the home market and increase the level of imports, thus reducing any surplus on visible trade. The extent to which resources switch to home demand will depend on the elasticity of domestic supply, i.e. how quickly domestic supply can meet increased home demand.

Allow its exchange rate to rise	That is, appreciate under floating rates, revalue under fixed exchange rates. Adjustment through the exchange rate mechanism involves changes in prices, so that the elasticities of demand for imports and exports will be crucial. If the demand for *imports* is elastic, then the total amount of foreign exchange paid out on imports will be greater at a lower domestic price, i.e. after appreciation (or revaluation) of the domestic currency; similarly, if the demand for *exports* is elastic, the amount of foreign exchange received for exports will be lower at the higher overseas price, i.e. after appreciation (or revaluation). The policy objective here is to increase total import payments and to decrease total export revenue.
Free imports from restrictions, and place restrictions on exports	Import restrictions, such as import quotas, restrict the volume of imports; *removal* of such restrictions will markedly increase imports. By the same reasoning, placing export quotas, especially if the demand for exports is inelastic, will quickly achieve a reduction in the volume of exports. However, some countries, for instance, those who produce and export oil, may prefer to place a tax on exports; this will not only reduce exports, but will at the same time benefit the national exchequer.
Reduce net 'invisible' earnings	This may be achieved by a variety of measures, such as giving grants to developing countries, or by encouraging residents to take holidays abroad and to send gifts to relatives and to charities overseas. Note that giving loans to developing countries will mean that interest on loans will increase the surplus on current account.
ADJUSTING A BALANCE OF PAYMENTS DEFICIT	A deficit country will need to adjust its current and/or capital accounts.
Adjustments on current account	A number of measures may be adopted:
1. Depreciation or devaluation of the exchange rate of the domestic currency	This means a fall in the exchange rate. Other things being equal, this will make imports expensive and therefore less competitive with domestic goods, and make exports more competitive in overseas markets. The extent of the reduction in imports and increase in exports will be determined by the relative elasticities of demand for imports and exports. If the price elasticity of demand for imports is elastic, i.e. if the percentage change in quantity of imports demanded divided by the percentage change in price of imports (consequent upon depreciation/devaluation)results in greater than one, then a rise in import price will cause a more than proportionate fall in the quantity of imports. The *value* of imports (quantity of imports × price) will then be less

than it was *before* the depreciation/devaluation. If, however, the price elasticity of demand for imports is inelastic, then depreciation/devaluation will cause the value of imports to be greater than it was prior to the fall in the exchange rate. A similar calculation will derive the price elasticity of demand for exports. Note that the calculation of the relative elasticities of demand for imports and exports is vital in order to determine precisely the extent to which the exchange value of the national currency must fall in order to achieve the desired level of import reduction and export expansion.

The factors which determine the demand elasticities for imports and exports are:

(a) the availability of close substitutes in terms of price and quality; such substitutes tend to make demand elastic;
(b) the time scale; in the short-term, both demand and supply tend to be less elastic than they are in the long-term.

If the *sum* of price E of D for exports and imports is *greater than one*, then a fall in the exchange rate will improve the balance of payments. In this case the Marshall-Lerner conditions are said to be fulfilled.

2. Deflationary policies

These may take the form of higher taxes and interest rates, tighter hire purchase regulations and constraints on bank lending, and reductions in government expenditure. The intention of all such policies is to reduce aggregate domestic demand, thereby reducing demand for imports as well. Further, as domestic demand is reduced, so will be the pressure on domestic prices, which may then fall; a lower rate of inflation will improve the competitiveness of exports and import substitutes. Note that deflationary policies to correct the current account deficits of member countries, are an integral part of IMF corrective measures.

3. Direct control measures

These may involve import controls or export subsidies. However, direct measures run the risk of retaliation by trading partners, and may contravene the rules and regulations of trade associations of which the deficit country may be a member, e.g. the General Agreement on Tariffs and Trade (GATT), the EEC, etc. The success of direct controls will largely depend upon the willing cooperation of trading partners.

4. Exchange controls

If stringently applied, these will place restrictions on the access to foreign currency by domestic residents. Buying foreign goods or foreign services has a negative effect on the current account; exchange controls may help reduce either or both, thereby reducing any Current Account deficit. However the effects of exchange controls on the Capital Account are often more dramatic, and it is to the capital account that we now turn.

Adjustments on capital account

A number of measures may be adopted:

(a) Higher interest rates encourage a greater inflow of currency; for example foreign short- and long-term investment may be attracted by higher returns. Higher interest rates may also discourage outflows of currency to other financial centres.

(b) Lower taxation on profits and an easier repatriation of capital and profits may attract even more foreign investment capital.

USEFUL APPLIED MATERIALS

THE STRUCTURE OF THE UK BALANCE OF PAYMENTS ACCOUNTS

According to the official statistics, provided regularly by the UK government, the main headings and sub-headings in the UK Balance of Payments Accounts are as shown in Table 3.

Table 3: UK balance of payments accounts

1. The Current account:

(a) Balance of trade
 Exports (visibles) (+)
 Imports (visibles) (−)

Visible trade balance (±)

(b) Invisibles
 Services (±)
 Interest, profits, dividends (±)
 Transfers (±)

Invisible trade balance (±)

Net current balance (±)

2. Investment and other capital flows:

Inward flow (+)	Outward flow (−)
Overseas investment in the UK:	Official long-term capital
private sector	UK private investment overseas
public sector	Import credits
Overseas currency borrowings by UK banks	Export credits
* Exchange reserves in sterling	
* Other external and money market liabilities in sterling	
Other transactions	
(+)	(−)

Net investment and other capital flows balance (±)

3. Total currency flow:

Net current balance (±)
Net investment and other capital flows balance (±)

Net currency flow (±)

4. The balancing item (±)

5. Official financing

Net currency flow $(\pm)$
Balancing item $(\pm)$

Balance for official financing $(\pm)$

Sources of official finance[a], [b]

(i) Overseas monetary authorities:
    International Monetary Fund $(+)$ or $(-)$
    Central banks $(+)$ or $(-)$
    Others $(+)$ or $(-)$

(ii) Foreign currency borrowings by
    The UK government $(+)$ or $(-)$
    Public bodies $(+)$ or $(-)$

(iii) The UK official reserves $(+)$ or $(-)$

Total official financing

Note:
(a) The balance of payments is an account, and like any other account it must balance: the function of official financing is to achieve that balance.
(b) In the context of official financing:
a '$-$' sign is a favourable entry because it reflects a positive net currency flow; a '$-$' sign here means either an increase in assets or a reduction in liabilities. For instance a balance of payments surplus can be used to increase official reserves or to pay off previous borrowing. a '$+$' sign is an unfavourable entry because it reflects a negative net currency flow; a '$+$' sign here means either a decrease in assets or an increase in liabilities. For instance a balance of payments deficit can be financed by running down official reserves or by extra borrowing.
* These two entries, under the Capital Account, are called 'Sterling Balances', and are highly sensitive to interest rate differentials and exchange rate movements. Holders of these balances are always seeking capital gains from such differentials and movements.

CURRENT ACCOUNT TRENDS IN THE UK

1979–1981

There was a small deficit on the current account balance (£0.5 billion) in 1979, which by 1981 had been turned into a record surplus (£7.2 billion). On the *visible trade balance* there was a substantial improvement over the years 1979–81, due to three main reasons:

1. The volume of imports, excluding oil, fell by nearly 5 per cent, due largely to the economic recession. The volume of exports, excluding oil, also fell, due to the world recession, but by only 3 per cent.
2. The UK *terms of trade* improved, i.e. export prices rose much more than import prices, largely due to an approximate 9 per cent appreciation of sterling's exchange value against all currencies. The causes for this appreciation were high domestic interest rates and the new status of sterling as a 'petro currency' at a time when oil prices were rising rapidly.

3. North Sea oil production rose rapidly, a deficit in the UK oil trade of over £700 million in 1979 was replaced by a surplus of over £3 billion in 1981.

<table>
<tr><td>

1981–85

</td><td>

Since 1981, the surplus on current account has steadily fallen, and in 1984 it was just about in balance. There are several reasons for the erosion of the current account surplus.

(a) In 1984 only, the miners' strike increased oil imports by about £2 billion.
(b) The UK economic recession bottomed in 1981; the subsequent increase in both consumer expenditure and investment in stockbuilding led to a rise in imports.
(c) The rise in the exchange rate of sterling up to 1981 caused a major deterioration in the UK export competitiveness. There is often a time lag of 18 months or so in the effect of the exchange rate on the value of exports and imports, so that the impact of the high exchange rate was still being felt several years later.
(d) Whilst the volume of imports increased by 16 per cent between 1981 and 1983, the volume of non-oil exports remained unchanged; the depressed state of world economic activity, especially in Europe, was an important cause of static exports.
(e) The terms of trade declined between 1981 and 1983, largely due to the depreciation of sterling.

The brunt of the deterioration in the visible trade balance has been borne by the manufacturing sector, which, for the first time during peacetime, was in deficit by £2.1 billion in 1983. The surplus on oil trade has continued to build up strongly, reaching £7.1 billion in 1984. In 1984, non-oil exports rose by about 7 per cent, but imports rose by 10 per cent. However, the decline in sterling's exchange rate may mean that the figures for 1985 will reveal no further deterioration in the UK balance of payments. Indeed, the latest Treasury forecasts suggest a current account surplus of about £2.5 billion in 1985.

</td></tr>
<tr><td>

THE SIGNIFICANCE OF NORTH SEA OIL

</td><td>

The exploration and development of North Sea oil has involved substantial overseas investment, mainly by foreign-owned oil companies. This represents a huge capital inflow. Subsequent interest, profits and dividends (IPD) payments on the overseas capital are of course debit items in the invisible account. In addition to IPD, imports of goods and services, e.g. the importing or hiring of drilling rigs, etc. are charges against the current account. However, undoubtedly the most important effect of North Sea oil production is on the increase in oil export revenues and on the reduction of the oil imports bill. In 1976, there was a deficit of £3.9 billion on UK oil trade; in 1984, there was a surplus of £7.1 billion. Clearly the increase in oil export earnings has been spectacular, but to put these earnings in true perspective, the outward IPD payments of £3 billion must be set against the surplus on UK oil trade to determine the overall effect of oil earnings on the UK balance of payments.

</td></tr>
</table>

Oil played a significant part in the rise of the sterling exchange rate in 1979 and 1980, and the subsequent loss of export competitiveness, resulting in a marked deterioration in UK manufacturing trade. A large oil surplus on the visible account has undoubtedly been detrimental to the UK's manufacturing trade.

The value of oil revenues in the UK balance of payments is crucially dependent on both the US dollar price of oil, because oil is priced in dollars, and on the sterling-dollar exchange rate. The cuts in oil price per barrel in 1984/85, in dollar terms, reduced the dollar value of UK oil revenues in the balance of payments. The fall in the world oil price pushed down the value of sterling, and sterling's heavy fall against the dollar pushed up the price per barrel that the UK receives in *sterling* terms. In 1980, the official price of oil was more than $32 a barrel; in 1981 it reached a peak of $33.76. Since then the official price has fallen, reaching $27.86 in October 1985. In November 1980, the sterling-dollar exchange rate was just under $2.40 to the pound, and in sterling terms a barrel of North Sea oil was worth only £13.34. In late 1981, with sterling around $1.90, a barrel was worth approximately £17.75. In January 1985, although the official *dollar* price was it its *lowest* for almost five years, the *sterling* value of each barrel was worth £25.50 to the UK exchequer. The plunge in the £–$ exchange rate in January 1985 coincided with North Sea oil production reaching a peak, causing a windfall in the UK's visible trade balance. The oil revenue figures for the fiscal year 1984/ 85 have been revised upwards by the authorities from £10 billion to £12 billion.

'INVISIBLES' AND CAPITAL ACCOUNT

Traditionally the UK invisibles balance performs well, and this trend has continued. The surpluses on 'services and IPD' have more than offset the usual deficits on 'transfers'.

Within the high and relatively stable surplus on 'services' over the past five years, rising earnings from financial services in particular have offset an emerging deficit in respect of sea transport and travel. However, the falls in the exchange rate of sterling during the first quarter of 1985 should lead to an improvement on tourism in 1985/86.

The 'transfers' account deficit in 1984 principally resulted from general government transactions such as grants to overseas countries, but most notably from net contributions to the EEC budget.

Although the 'IPD' account has shown a fairly steady overall surplus in recent years, yet this conceals important changes. The IPD earnings of foreign oil companies have risen to over £3 billion, against the UK earnings on IPD of £3 billion, largely due to the abolition of exchange controls in 1979. Private UK overseas investment has been a major counterpart to the large current account surplus of recent years. By the end of 1984, the net external assets of the UK private sector were approximately £70 billion, compared to less than £10 billion in 1979. The UK capital outflow is now producing substantial IPD earnings, which boost the UK Current Account balance, and which will be a major support to the balance of payments when North Sea oil production declines. However, the outflow of capital has kept the sterling exchange rate down; although this has helped to limit the deterioration in competitiveness, it has worsened the problem facing the authorities in stabilizing the exchange rate of sterling against the dollar, despite a 4.5 per cent increase in UK interest rates in January 1985; the fear is that a low exchange rate may help fuel a resurgence of inflation, via high import prices.

RECENT EXAMINATION QUESTIONS	The questions on this topic tend to be repetitive. The following six questions from recent Monetary Economics papers are good examples of the types of question which are commonly asked. Try to spend ten minutes or so in preparing your own outline answers to each question before reading the outline answers provided.
Question 1.	(a) Distinguish between the concepts of balance of (visible) trade and terms of trade. (b) Analyse how changes in the terms of trade help to determine a country's balance of trade.
Question 2.	Is a deficit on a country's visible trade account necessarily of concern to its government? Discuss the ways in which a deficit may be corrected.
Question 3.	In what sense does a country's balance of payments accounts always balance? How will the operation of a truly floating exchange rate regime affect the balance for official financing?
Question 4.	Assess the effects on the UK balance of payments (both current and capital accounts) of the development and production of North Sea oil.
Question 5.	The figures below are taken from the annual balance of payments of Ruritania. Prepare: (a) Ruritania's balance of visible trade. (b) Ruritania's balance of payments on current account. Do these figures support the contention that Ruritania is a developing economy, and not highly industrialized? Give reasons for your answer.

	Million Rurits
Banking earnings (net)	− 30
Capital movements (net flow)	+ 1,280
Insurance earnings (net)	− 20
Interest paid abroad	+ 30
Manufactured goods:	
exports (fob)	+120
imports (fob)	− 2,000
Raw materials and fuel:	
exports (fob)	+ 3,000
imports (fob)	− 1,000
Shipping earnings (net)	− 80
Tourists earnings (net)	+ 100

Note: There were no changes in Ruritania's official reserves during the year.

Question 6.

What do you understand by the 'invisibles' section of a country's balance of payments accounts? Assess the importance of and recent influences on the invisibles account of the United Kingdom.

OUTLINE ANSWERS

Answer 1.

(a) Balance of visible trade: the value of exports *minus* the value of imports of goods for a given period. The balance can be in surplus or deficit.

- Terms of trade. Changes in export prices expressed as a percentage of changes in import prices of a country during a given period; then expressed as an index, with some base year = 100.
- The concept of terms of trade measures the purchasing power of a fixed 'bundle' of goods exported in terms of goods imported. Terms of trade refer to multilateral, not bilateral, trade.

(b) The effect of changes in terms of trade on the balance of trade:
- Elasticities of demand for exports and imports are crucial:
  (i) if elastic, then total receipts will be greater at lower prices. This means that a **lower** price for exports will help raise export earnings and a **higher** price for imports will help cut import spending – i.e. unfavourable terms of trade will help the balance of payments.
  (ii) if inelastic, then total receipts will be greater at higher prices. A higher export price/lower import price will now help the balance of payments – i.e. favourable terms of trade.

Answer 2.

A deficit on visible trade is not necessarily of concern to the government. Of importance are:
- the position on the current (i.e. visibles + invisibles) and capital accounts in the balance of payments.

- the sign and size of the **overall** balance for official financing; only if this is negative will there be a need for official financing via running down reserves and/or borrowing overseas.
- Whether the deficit on visible trade is temporary or permanent.
- the stage of development for the national economy.

The main ways of correcting (not financing) a balance of trade deficit:
(i)   By devaluation (fixed exchange rates) or depreciation (floating rates) of the exchange rate. Success depends on: adequate price elasticities of demand for exports and imports (**sum** must be >1, i.e. Marshall – Lerner conditions fulfilled); no competitive devaluation or depreciation; no offsetting increase in wages, profit margins, or indirect taxes.
(ii) By deflationary policies: higher taxes and interest rates, and less attractive hire purchase terms; more attractive saving schemes; a credit squeeze.
(iii) By direct measures: import controls; export subsidies. Success will depend upon no retaliatory measures by trading partners.

Answer 3.

The balance of payments accounts always balance in an *accounting* sense: balance of payments accounts include visible trade balance, 'invisible' balance and the balance of investments and other capital flows; the sum of these, along with the balancing item, produces the balance for official financing.
- The value of official financing will be equal, but opposite in sign (plus or minus), to the balance for official financing; this preserves the accounting identity.
- Under freely floating rates, the balance for official financing should be zero, because the movements in the exchange rate should be such as exactly to counterbalance the deficit/surplus position on current and capital accounts; there may of course be time lags before, say, the fall in exchange rate can eliminate a deficit in the balance for official financing.

Answer 4.

The effects of the development and production of North Sea oil on the UK balance of payment are, in approximate time sequence:
- On the capital account:
  (i) Inflow of foreign capital to finance exploration and development.
  (ii) As the UK becomes self-sufficient in oil it becomes more attractive for foreign investment (i.e. as petro-currency, its currency is believed to be stronger – at least while oil prices are high).
- On the current account:
  (i) Imports of equipment cause some worsening in the visible balance.
  (ii) Interest payments on foreign capital reduce net receipts on invisibles.

(iii) As production begins, oil imports fall, visible trade balance improves considerably; eventually oil exports may arise, further improving the visible trade balance.

(iv) Foreign oil companies may remit dividends to overseas shareholders or profits to their overseas headquarters, thus increasing the debits in the invisible section of the accounts.

(v) Increase in investment in the UK raises the exchange value of sterling, imports increase, exports decrease and the UK industrial base shrinks.

● Since North Sea oil is located in the UK, although offshore, oil tax revenues are domestic transfers, and do not affect the UK balance of payments.

Answer 5.

	Dr. (million Rurits)	Cr. (million Rurits)
(a) Balance of visible trade		
Exports of manufactures		120
Exports of raw materials/fuel		3,000
Imports of manufactures	2,000	
Imports of raw material/fuel	1,000	
	3,000	3,120
Visible trade surplus		120 m. Rurits
(b) Invisibles		
Banking	30	
Insurance	20	
Interest paid	1,400	
Interest received		30
Shipping	80	
Tourism		100
	1,530	130

Deficit on invisibles   1400 m. Rurits

Balance of payments on current account = visibles + invisibles
$$= +120 - 1\,400 \text{ m. Rurits}$$
$$= -1\,280 \text{ m. Rurits}$$

Capital inflow was 1280 million Rurits, because official reserves were unchanged.

Ruritania is a developing country because:

● greater reliance on exports of raw materials and less on exports of manufactures;

● low earnings from commercial services;

● large interest payment on current account and heavy borrowings on capital account;

● sizeable tourist earnings suggest unspoilt countryside, 'golden' beaches, lower price level, etc.

Answer 6.

The 'invisibles' section of a country's balance of payments shows:

- The net receipts or payments in respect of commercial services, interest, profit, dividends, and tourism in the private sector.
- Overseas grants and aid, by the government.
- Transfer payments: private (to relatives abroad); government (e.g. the UK payments to the EEC).

The importance of recent influences on the invisibles account of the UK:

- In the earlier 1980s, the relatively strong sterling exchange rate had a negative effect on inward travel and a positive effect on outward travel (i.e. deterioration of tourism section of the account).
- A major portion of investment in the North Sea oil was by overseas oil companies, which led to large payments abroad of profits and dividends.
- The abolition of exchange control led to an increase in investments overseas as large institutions broadened their portfolio of asset holdings. This resulted in increased receipts in the UK of interest, profits and dividends.
- A sharp deterioration in the transfer account, despite rebates, because of payments by the UK to the EEC.
- The heavy fall in the exchange rate of sterling at the end of 1984 and in early 1985 has had a positive inward and negative outward travel effect.

A TUTOR'S ANSWER

The following question has been chosen for the specimen answer because it is the question most frequently asked on the topic of the Balance of Payments. You will notice from the answer plan that it is essential that you avoid confusing the two elements of the question.

Question

In which ways can a deficit on the current account of a country's balance of payments be:
(a) financed;
(b) rectified?

Answer plan

- Definition of the 'current account' within the balance of payments (briefly).
- How does a deficit on current account occur (briefly)?
  (a) Deficit may be financed by:
  – private capital inflows;
  – sources of official finance.
  (b) Deficit may be corrected by:
  – devaluation/depreciation;
  – deflation;
  – direct controls.

Specimen answer

The current account of a country's balance of payments consists of:

(i)   *The balance of trade*. This is the difference between the value of goods exported and the value of goods imported; this balance may be positive ($+$) or negative ($-$).

(ii) *The invisibles balance*. This shows the net receipts ($+$) or payments ($-$) in respect of services, transfer payments, and interest, profit and dividends.

A deficit on the current account occurs when (a) + (b) is negative. It implies that the country is a debtor on its external current account transactions with its trading partners, and suggests a poor performance in buying and selling goods and services with the rest of the world.

A current account may be *financed* by:

1.   Private capital inflows. If the country in question offers good prospects for high profitability, then overseas private *long-term* investment, in foreign currencies, will be attracted into the country. The long-term overseas investment may be direct investment into factories, equipment, etc. or it could be indirect portfolio investment, in purchasing stocks and shares in the country. If the country offers opportunities of interest-rate differential gains or capital gains due to exchange rate movements, it may attract *short-term* private capital (hot money). The net receipts of foreign currencies from long-term and short-term foreign capital will help reduce the deficit on current account.

2.   If the current account deficit is not wholly financed by the inflow of private capital, then the government of the country will need to tap the three main sources of official finance:

(a)   transactions with overseas monetary authorities and the International Monetary Fund to obtain supplies of the currencies needed;

(b)   borrowing, by the public sector, of foreign currency in the international financial market;

(c)   reducing official reserves of the country.

The country may take three main measures, singly or in a 'mix', to rectify the deficit on its current account.

1.   By devaluation or depreciation of the exchange rate of its currency. This would make exports cheaper and imports more expensive. The effectiveness of this approach depends on:

(a)   the relative price elasticities for exports overseas and for imports at home; the greater the **sum** of these elasticities, the more favourable the impact of a fall in the exchange rate on the balance of payments

(b)   no competitive devaluation or depreciation by trading partners. There will tend to be a time lag of 18 months or so before the fall in the exchange rate has its full impact on export sales and import purchases ('J' curve effect).

2. Using deflationary policies (increasing tax rates and interest rates, credit squeeze, etc.), will reduce aggregate domestic demand in general, thereby dampening the demand for imports. Furthermore, deflationary policies will tend to lower the domestic rate of inflation which, in turn, will improve the competitiveness of its exports and its production of import substitutes.

3. By using direct controls, involving either import tariffs and other controls, or export subsidies. However, direct measures run the risk of retaliation, and may prove to be self-defeating. The success of direct controls will depend upon the willing cooperation of the trading partners.

A STEP FURTHER

The topic of balance of payments has comparatively less direct bearing on Monetary Economics than other topics in the syllabus. However, it is an important area for examination questions. You are expected to be able to appreciate *recent* influences on the constituent parts of the UK balance of payments accounts. You need to keep abreast of developments by reading current banking journals, financial reports, The Institute of Bankers *Examiners' Reports* and *Updating Notes*. The UK government releases a monthly balance of payments statement, which is the basis for comments by the quality press, television and radio programmes. Look out for this media coverage of the monthly balance of payments statement.

Chapter 8

Foreign exchange rates and markets

- Understand the workings of the foreign exchange markets.
- Understand the basis of bilateral and multilateral trade and the need for foreign currencies.
- Be aware of the general operation of the foreign exchange markets.
- Understand the domestic and external factors which determine exchange rate movements.
- Evaluate the different types of exchange rate policies from fixed (IMF system) to free floating and the various compromises.
- Examine the development of the European Monetary System, particularly post-1979.
- Appreciate the relationship between exchange rates and interest rates.

GETTING STARTED

'Foreign exchange' generally means any currency other than your own. The 'foreign exchange rate' of a currency implies the exchange value of the currency (its price) in terms of other currencies and, like any other price, it is determined by the supply of and demand for the currency of the 'foreign exchange markets'. Foreign exchange (forex) markets provide an international system of buying and selling claims to currencies immediately (spot) and in the future (forward) involving a world-wide group of banks, brokers, commercial companies and other financial institutions.

The need for foreign exchange (i.e. foreign currencies) arises for many reasons. A country, its business companies and citizens may require foreign currencies to pay the purchase price for imported goods and services, to invest in other countries, to provide for its tourists going abroad and to sustain the sending of gifts and other payments overseas.

If the bilateral (between two currencies) and multilateral (among all currencies) exchange rates are absolutely fixed on the forex markets, then there will be certainty in trade payments; for instance as regards imports, it will be clear how much the buyer in the domestic country needs to pay in terms of his currency, and how much the seller in the foreign country will receive in terms of his currency. However, the domestic purchasing power of the currencies does not remain static, mainly due to inflation rate differentials and major changes in the supply and demand of currencies (e.g. via balance of payments deficits and surpluses and consequent changes in international indebtedness). These factors put too much pressure upon the central banks to hold the absolutely fixed exchange rate parities. Hence absolute certainty may have to be replaced by the compromise of relative certainty, i.e. the absolutely fixed exchange rate system is replaced by one in which there is some movement of the exchange rate between specified upper and lower limits. However, international circumstances may make it difficult even to uphold a system with this degree of flexibility in exchange rates. If so, then the monetary authorities of individual countries have no option but to allow the exchange value of their respective currencies to be determined by supply and demand on the forex markets, i.e. to accept a system of freely floating exchange rates. The authorities may still intervene in a free exchange rate system, buying or selling currencies to affect the exchange rate. Such a 'managed' system can be compared with a 'pure' system in which no intervention takes place.

The international monetary system, whether of fixed, managed or pure floating exchange rates, exists to facilitate international trade and the settlement of debt; it is the international counterpart of the national monetary systems of the trading countries.

ESSENTIAL PRINCIPLES

THE BASIS OF BILATERAL AND MULTILATERAL TRADE

The objective of *bilateral* trade is to regulate trade with each single country in such a way as to secure an exact balance of payments with it. The need for bilateral trade arises where one currency cannot be easily converted into other currencies, so that the earnings from trade with one country cannot be used to pay for goods and services imported from other countries; the only way to pay for imports is then by exports. Bilateral trade, therefore, is completely controlled by inter-governmental agreements.

Under *multilateral* trade, a country aims, not at exactly offsetting imports and exports with each single country, but at a general balance of trade. Multilateral trade is not possible without the 'convertibility' of one currency into other currencies. Only then can countries use their surplus earnings from one country to offset deficits with other countries, so that a multilateral trade system becomes possible. The basis of multilateral trade is the theory of *comparative advantage*.

Under this theory countries specialize in those economic activities in which they have a relative advantage in terms of efficiency over other countries. Specialization, based on comparative advantage, reduces costs of production, and international trade not only passes on this advantage to consumers in other countries, but also widens their choice of goods and services.

Multilateral trade makes possible international investment, so that investors in one country can take advantage of national differences in yields on investments and can reduce overall investment risk by diversifying their investment portfolios. Investment capital can then flow to countries with projects offering the highest projected returns; these may be low cost centres of production, which can then expand at the expense of other countries where costs are higher. Thus multilateral trade, unhindered by tariffs, exchange controls and other artificial barriers, can lead to an efficient, worldwide use of resources.

International trade and investment is therefore only possible if suitable means are available for international payments. Most international trade nowadays is settled by using national currencies, either the currency of the exporter or one of a limited number of currencies that command general confidence and are widely accepted in international payments.

OPERATION OF FOREIGN EXCHANGE MARKETS

Traders and investors must be able to buy and sell national currencies if they are to make international payments. The forex markets have developed to allow this. Trading in these markets determines the rates at which one currency can be exchanged for others. The forex markets play a central role in facilitating international trade, and their smooth functioning is essential for the expansion of trade and investment.

National currencies are bought and sold in major financial centres, e.g. New York, Singapore, Hong Kong, Tokyo, Frankfurt, Paris and London. London is one of the largest centres of activity with several hundred institutions, mainly banks, dealing in foreign exchange, and with more currencies actively traded than in any other major centre. Foreign exchange dealers in forex markets do not meet in a particular location but keep in touch via telephone, telex, and other more sophisticated forms of electronic communication. Exchange rates adjust continually, depending on the balance between orders for buying and selling currencies, and instant communications, combined with extreme competitiveness, ensure that exchange rates in different financial centres keep closely in step.

Inconsistencies between exchange rates, if they appeared, would quickly be exploited by a process known as *arbitrage*. This involves buying currencies in the financial centres where they are quoted more cheaply and selling them on forex markets where they are quoted at a better rate. The overall result of arbitrage is that the exchange rates soon adjust and come into line in each centre until there is no incentive for arbitrage (see below).

There are two basic types of foreign exchange transactions; spot and forward. Currency is bought and sold for prompt delivery (i.e. two working days hence) in the *spot* market; currency is bought and sold for delivery at a specified future date in the *forward* market. Forward contracts can reduce or eliminate the risk of adverse movements in exchange rates, which may upset the profitability of importers and exporters. The extent to which importers and exporters choose to avoid exchange risk by using the forward market, depends partly on their expectations of future movements in spot rates compared to the cost of covering forward, and partly on their own attitude to risk.

Whereas arbitrage exploits the inconsistencies between exchange rates quoted in various centres, *speculation* aims at profit-making from the expected movements in exchange rates; for example, by selling a currency on the spot market in the hope of buying it later at a lower rate of exchange, or by buying a currency on the spot market in the hope of selling it later at a higher rate. Like arbitrage, speculation on forex markets hastens the adjustments in exchange rates by anticipating changes; thus, in this sense, both arbitrage and speculation are market forces which help forex markets regain equilibrium quickly, so that it can be argued that these market forces serve an economic purpose. However, in recent years, the amount of speculative balances have increased substantially, both in volume and volatility. Movements of such balances in response to anticipated changes in exchange rates in the forex markets can *overcompensate* for any possible degree of non-alignment, thereby causing much greater short-term changes in exchange rates. This will place intense pressures on the central banks of the countries whose currencies are the object of speculation, whether for appreciation or depreciation.

THE DETERMINATION OF EXCHANGE RATES

Since the exchange rate of a currency is its price on the forex markets in terms of other currencies, it is determined by demand and supply conditions in the forex markets: instant communications and extreme competitiveness among the forex markets make them almost perfect markets. The demand for, and supply of, a country's currency are derived from the country's balance of payments position; if it is a surplus country, i.e. if the value of its exports of goods and services and capital inflows (demand for its currency) is greater than the value of its imports of goods and services and capital outflows (supply of its currency) then the demand for its currency will be rising relative to the supply. The forex markets will then quote the currency at a higher exchange rate. On the other hand, if it is a deficit country, the supply of its currency will be rising relative to the demand and the forex markets will quote a lower exchange value for it. There are two main theories which seek to explain the determination of exchange rates: one relates to the current account, and the other to the capital account.

The purchasing power parity (PPP) theory

In its original form the theory states that the equilibrium exchange rate between one currency and another is that rate which equalizes the domestic purchasing powers of the two currencies. If, for example, £1 buys the same amount of goods and services in the UK as do 10 francs in France, then, according to PPP theory, the equilibrium exchange rate must be £1 = 10 francs. If this were not the case, there would be strong incentives to import goods from the 'cheaper' country, which would lead to a deficit on the current accunt for the 'expensive' country; as the supply of its currency increased in settling its current account deficit, the forex markets would mark down its exchange rate. The incentive for importing goods and services from the 'cheaper' country would only disappear when the sterling/franc exchange rate becomes equal to £1 = 10 francs.

The PPP theory was originally developed to explain the values of exchange rates in the long run. However, there are many problems associated with this theory in its original form. For instance, the theory ignores transport and insurance costs and import duties. More importantly, it depends on the extent to which the goods and services involved may enter into international trade; there are many goods and services which are traded internally, but which *cannot* be traded internationally, e.g. houses, haircuts. The theory has been refined to take account of differences in patterns of consumption and levels of income in different countries. Nevertheless, the problem of devising baskets of goods and services which reflect common consumption patterns in different countries yet which only include goods which are traded internationally, has limited the usefulness of the theory in predicting exchange rates. Since the relative costs and prices of *non-traded* goods and services can vary between countries, a comparison of *general* price levels is not therefore a reliable way of determining the exchange rate equilibrium.

However, the theory has a broad relevance in times of differing inflation rates in the domestic economies of trading partners. If a country's inflation rate significantly exceeds that of its trading partners then, generally speaking, its exports will become uncompetitive at any given exchange rate; as a result it may encounter balance of payment problems, and, in a floating system, the exchange rate will fall.

The portfolio balance theory

This theory emphasizes the importance of interest rate differentials in the financial centres, and their impact on international investment and speculative flows, as a major determinant of exchange rates. It is assumed that large sophisticated investors are aware of interest rate differentials and move funds to take advantage of higher yields; also that they seek to reduce overall investment risks by diversifying their portfolios. The inflow of these funds into financial centres offering higher yield increases the demand for the currencies of such centres, so that the exchange rates of these currencies rise on the forex markets.

DIFFERENT TYPES OF EXCHANGE RATE SYSTEMS

National monetary policies of the trading partners are to some extent interdependent, on account of the exchange rate links between their currencies. Therefore changes in national monetary policies, even if in pursuit of internal objectives, put pressure on the international exchange rate system in operation.

There are two main exchange rate systems, absolutely fixed and freely floating.

Absolutely fixed exchange rates

The central bank of each country is obliged to intervene to increase or decrease the supply of its currency on the forex markets, so that its exchange rate is maintained at a predetermined exchange parity with certain other currencies.

Freely floating exchange rates

The exchange value of each currency is determined, not by the monetary authorities, but by the market forces of supply and demand for each currency on the forex markets. In a 'pure' float, the central banks take no action, whatever the exchange values quoted for their respective currencies.

In between these two extremes, there are a number of compromise arrangements:

(a) *Fluctuation limits around parity values* – the international trading community agrees that exchange rates can vary within specific bands either side of an agreed central parity; the central banks only intervening on the forex markets to ensure that the foreign exchange value of their currencies remains within the agreed bands.

(b) *'Dirty' floating* – in which the monetary authorities profess to follow freely floating exchange rates policies, yet intervene, behind the scenes, to limit the fluctuations in the exchange rates of their currencies to such levels as are most beneficial for their own economies. This is sometimes called a 'managed' float.

(c) *Crawling peg* – the monetary authorities, instead of declaring and maintaining a fixed parity, allow the parities to adjust from time to time, i.e. a system of 'gliding' fixed parities.

(d) *Direct foreign exchange control* – each central bank states the terms and conditions for the release of foreign exchange. An extreme type of direct control is 'counter trading', i.e. all foreign trade transactions are undertaken as purely bilateral barter arrangements.

FIXED VERSUS FLOATING EXCHANGE RATES

If the fixed exchange regime is to function satisfactorily, it is essential that all countries under this regime should ensure that they do not let their interest rates, inflation rates and monetary expansion rates move too far out of line with those prevailing elsewhere within the regime. Those countries which are unwilling or unable to abide by the strict discipline of fixed exchange rates will find their price levels rising above those of the countries which *are* adhering to such discipline;

their exports will become less, and imports more, competitive, leading to rising balance of payments deficits year by year. In order to defend the fixed exchange rate parities, the central banks of these countries will have to continue buying their own currencies on an increasing scale, spending their foreign exchange reserves, until their reserves fall dangerously low. The monetary authorities may then be forced to devalue their currencies by declaring lower exchange parities, in order to avoid continuous intervention on the forex markets. There is a stigma attached to 'devaluing' under a fixed exchange rate regime, which countries under such a regime will try to avoid at almost any cost. The strongest argument in favour of fixed exchange rates is that, since currencies will be accepted at known and fixed exchange rates, there will be certainty in international payments and receipts. Fixed exchange rates will eliminate exchange risks and thereby promote international trade and investment.

With fixed exchange rates, however, inflation in the economies of some trading partners will be 'imported' into other, non-inflation, economies, unless the demand for imports is relatively price elastic, and cheaper domestic import substitutes are preferred.

In stark contrast to the fixed exchange rate regime, there is the freely floating system. With freely floating, market determined, exchange rates, it is claimed that there will be less need for official reserves; this follows since (a) there will be no exchange parities to defend, and (b) balance of payments' imbalances should be automatically corrected by movements in exchange rates. Furthermore, with no fixed regime rules to obey, national governments will be able to pursue independent domestic economic policies, aimed at higher growth and employment. Individual economies will be insulated against 'imported' inflation. The economies with the higher inflation rates will tend to experience an automatic fall in their exchange rates. This will reduce their export prices, making imports into the non-inflation economies somewhat cheaper.

However, these theoretical advantages of floating exchange rates do not always fully materialize. For instance, if the adjustment of balance of payments imbalances is to be automatic, it is essential that the elasticities of demand for imports and exports are sufficiently high to support the automatic adjustment process. Again, even though there is no exchange rate parity to defend, countries are not always free to follow independent monetary policies. For example, rapid growth may bring about higher imports and a fall in the exchange rate; even if this raises import prices and curbs the growth in imports, it may so stimulate domestic inflation that the 'cost' of this policy is still too high, despite balance of payments equilibrium.

There will be less need for official reserves or international borrowing only if the exchange rates are *truly* floating. If floating is 'dirty', i.e. managed, there will still be a need for official reserves so that the authorities can intervene on forex markets.

The principal weakness of floating rates is that they might discourage international trade and investment. It is not so much the flexibility in current exchange rates that discourages trade and investment; rather it is the uncertainty about future exchange rates which might have this effect. If, however, movements in exchange rates were easily predicted, then traders and investors could take them into account when planning overseas business and investment.

USEFUL APPLIED MATERIALS

THE PROBLEMS OF THE INTERNATIONAL CURRENCY SYSTEMS SINCE BRETTON WOODS

Under the Bretton Woods arrangements, most countries operated on fixed exchange rates for 25 years. Individual governments set international values (parities) for their currencies, and then intervened, by buying and selling them, to preserve those values.

The system suffered from two main drawbacks:

1. The fixed rates of the currencies related to their 'nominal' and not to their 'real' values, i.e. their values adjusted for international inflation differentials. Therefore, if one country's costs of production rose faster than similar costs in other countries, its ability to compete gradually decreased and its trade deficit grew. To restore balance, its exchange rate needed to fall. Conversely, those countries which had a lower inflation rate than the rest of the world developed balance of payments surpluses; their exchange rate needed to rise to cut their competitive advantage and trade surplus. In practice, it proved easier to get a deficit country to devalue than it did to get a surplus country to revalue.

2. As it became obvious that an exchange rate would devalue/revalue, so an easy capital gain could be made by selling the currency to be devalued and buying the currency to be revalued. Such switching by speculators on the forex markets usually involved official losses, as the central banks concerned tried to resist the market pressures by buying or selling their currencies. Sometimes official intervention in the markets could not stop changes in exchange rates, so that private gains were made at the expense of huge official losses.

In the 1960s, as inflation rates rose and became more variable, the need for exchange rate changes grew. During the same decade, the volume of speculative money balances grew as well, thus making the work of the central banks in maintaining their exchange values almost impossible. The fixed exchange rate system, as organized under Bretton Woods arrangements, clearly had to be modified.

In 1971, under the Smithsonian Agreement, the Bretton Woods rules for fixed exchange rates were changed: currencies were allowed to fluctuate within a 2¼ per cent band around their central exchange rate, rather than 1 per cent as initially allowed under the Bretton Woods arrangement. However, this extra flexibility within the regime of fixed rates perhaps came too late, and it failed to shift the balance sufficiently in favour of central banks. The system had become unworkable.

By March 1973, most major currencies openly abandoned the

official fixed rates and either began to float against each other or to link themselves to one currency (many are still linked to the dollar) or to a basket of currencies. The subsequent floating has almost always been 'managed': central banks have *not* abrogated their responsibilities towards the exchange value of their currencies and have intervened in the markets, sometimes on a larger scale than they did under Bretton Woods, to defend the existing rates. Despite these official interventions, currencies have fluctuated considerably.

INFLUENCES CAUSING EXCHANGE RATE MOVEMENTS

Despite the purchasing power parity theory – which states that competition in trade will tend to compensate for differences in national inflation rates, i.e. that exchange rates will be constant in real terms – there is litle evidence that real exchange rates do in fact tend to be stable. Real exchange rates have varied markedly over both short and long periods. It may be that in the *very long term*, say 15 to 20 years, the forces represented by the purchasing power parity theory may become dominant and create stability in real exchange rates, but it is a largely unproven hypothesis.

It is likely that some of the longer term movements in real exchange rates which occurred between 1972 and 1980 were partly due to a movement towards more diversified reserve currency portfolios (see Ch. 9), following the collapse of the US dollar-dominated Bretton Woods regime. It is also possible that the transfers of wealth towards OPEC (Organization of Petroleum Exporting Countries), due largely to the huge oil price increases, had a significant impact on global currency preferences: a few major oil producers were now able to place, or withdraw, huge sums in financial centres and currencies of their choice. For the UK, the advent of North Sea oil certainly raised the demand for sterling from the mid 1970s.

The comparison of data on various countries' balance of payments positions indicates that changes in the current account balances have frequently influenced exchange rate movements in the short term. This would suggest that the current account does have an impact on the longer-term value of a country's exchange rate.

Short-term movements in exchange rates appear to have been linked to relative interest rates, but this relationship has sometimes been positive and sometimes negative. A *positive* relationship has prevailed most frequently in recent years, as monetary authorities have followed an interest rate policy directed more towards domestic rather than external objectives (except for the 4.5 per cent rise in interest rates in January 1985 in the UK). A high relative interest rate has tended to raise the exchange rate of the currency in question. Where there has been a *negative* relationship, e.g. where a high relative interest rate has been associated with the exchange rate remaining constant or falling (as has been happening in the UK in 1985), it has perhaps been due to *expectations* of a still greater rise (or fall) in interest rates.

In addition to the above influences on exchange rate movements, there are other influences, such as the stance of fiscal policy (expansionary or deflationary) and the level of economic activity. However, these influences will reflect themselves in both the balance of payments current accounts and in interest rates.

In summary, then, exchange rates may be influenced by relative inflation rates, by relative current account positions, by relative interest rates, by relative fiscal/monetary stances, and by a range of other factors, such as the degree of intervention on forex markets. In the forex markets, though, it is often merely 'expectations' as regards one of the above that causes movements.

THE EUROPEAN MONETARY SYSTEM AND ITS ORIGIN

It became clear to the European countries that despite the wider fluctuation bands around central rates introduced in 1971 under the Smithsonian agreement, the fixed exchange rate system could not be saved. In an attempt to keep the narrowest possible exchange rate fluctuations among themselves, ten European countries moved in the opposite direction in April 1972. They introduced narrower cross exchange rates against each other's currencies (1 ⅛ per cent either way), while maintaining the wider band (2¼ per cent) against the US dollar. This arrangement was quickly nicknamed the 'Snake in the Tunnel'. The Snake aimed at reducing uncertainty as regards the exchange rates of the members by limiting the extent of fluctuations against each other. This took place at a time when most major currencies were beginning to show signs of abandoning the Bretton Woods/Smithsonian arrangements prior to floating against each other. However, balance of payments imbalances, largely due to the oil crisis in 1973, caused volatile exchange rate fluctuations, making it very difficult to maintain par values within the narrow bands of the Snake. Despite currencies entering and leaving the Snake at various times, it remained in existence until 1979, when the Snake was replaced by the European Monetary System (EMS).

The EMS

The EMS was established by the Brussels Resolution dated 5 December 1978, signed by all EEC countries, and was implemented on 13 March 1979. The objectives of the EMS were to combat the international monetary instability caused by the weakness of the US dollar in the 1970s, to establish a zone of monetary stability in Europe, to assist in drawing together the monetary and economic policies of EEC countries and to promote inter-community trade by stabilizing exchange rates.

The EMS has two major elements:

1. An exchange rate intervention system which attempts to preserve stability between the different currencies participating in it. It organizes exchange rate relationships between the participants according to a system of stable parities, but ones which can be adjusted when necessary. It allows for periodic realignments and permits margins of fluctuation between currencies. Thus the

EMS is a 'movable peg' exchange rate system for the participating currencies.

The heart of the EMS is the *European Currency Unit* (ECU), which is a weighted 'basket' of ten EEC currencies, of which two, sterling and the Greek drachma, are not members of the EMS; the weight of each currency is determined by the economic strength of the country concerned. Each currency participating in the exchange rate mechanism (ERM) of the EMS has an ECU-related central rate, and these values determine a grid of bilateral central rates between the members. Every country must maintain a margin of + or − 2¼ per cent on either side of its bilateral rate. Italy is an exception, because of the weakness of the lira, and at present its intervention limits are roughly 6 per cent on either side of its central rate. If a currency reaches its upper or lower bilateral intervention point in relation to another currency, its central bank must intervene on the forex market to buy or sell its currency for ECUs, to raise or lower its exchange rate respectively. The EMS supplements the compulsory intervention rules with a 'divergence indicator', which is based on the ECU as the common numeraire, and which gives countries a forewarning that their currencies are getting out of line from the Community average. If a currency moves to 75 per cent of its maximum spread of divergence in relation to the Community average, then it is an 'early warning' to the country concerned to take corrective monetary and/or fiscal measures before the compulsory intervention points are reached. Therefore all participant currencies are pegged against the ECU directly and against each other indirectly. Clearly ERM is the cornerstone of the EMS, and is vital to the achievement of EMS objectives. The UK and Greece have not as yet joined the ERM of the EMS.

2. Each member country of the EEC (including the UK) makes 20 per cent of gold and dollar reserves available to the European Monetary Cooperation Fund (EMCF) in return for ECUs. EMCF is empowered to lend up to 25 billion ECUs to member countries confronting balance of payments problems.
Note: While intervention is carried out through national currencies, debts are settled in ECUs. Thus EMS is an improvement on the old Snake arrangement which was simply an exchange rate agreement.

The staunch critics of the EMS point to its lack of success in achieving fully many of its objectives. For instance, critics question how the EMS can bring about a zone of exchange rate stability when, in its first six and a half years of existence – March 1979 to October 1985 – there were eight (four of them major) realignments of exchange rate parities! Due to a lack of convergence of economic policies of member states, there have been differences in inflation rates and in balance of payments performance among member countries; the fact that such differences continue to exist may suggest further realignments. The

EMS has, therefore, failed in leading the member states towards the objective of European Monetary Union, in which the economic policies of the members are fully harmonized. The ECU has not become a major 'reserve' asset for the EEC countries, and the EMCF has not developed, as was expected, into a fully fledged European Monetary Fund (on the pattern of the International Monetary Fund).

The supporters of the EMS counter-argue, emphasizing the degree of success the EMS has been able to achieve in moving towards its objectives. For instance, it has survived, despite the eight realignments, because it has an in-built flexibility, which the IMF did not possess and which caused the downfall of the latter. Despite differentials in rates of inflation and in balance of payment outcomes, there have been no further realignments since March 1983, a significant success in view of the traumatic happenings on the forex markets during 1985, largely caused by the strength of the US dollar against all EMS currencies. The member states are *beginning* to accept the need for convergence of their economic policies, e.g. French monetary policy is now much closer to the monetary policies of Germany and the UK.

It is true that the EMCF has not developed in importance as was expected, and that the hopes of it becoming a fully-fledged European Monetary Fund have been shelved indefinitely. However, the ECU has remained stable, due largely to the stabilizing influence of the EMS, despite massive exchange rate swings and interest rate fluctuations. The ECU has gradually become a fully-fledged financial instrument used by banks, businessmen and governments for accounting, investment, savings and payments purposes. The ECU is not far short of becoming a reserve asset for the EEC countries and is now a major currency for loans and bond issues. Companies, too, now often insist on paying or being paid in ECUs. This removes the risk of one currency fluctuating far from the other currencies – a weighted average of currencies is inherently more stable than just one currency.

The EMS, unlike the IMF, is not an institution in its own right. It has no real teeth to force member states to pursue some prescribed monetary and fiscal policies. A basic precondition for the successful operation of the EMS is that there is convergence of economic policies and performance of member countries; *how* they achieve this convergence largely rests with their own respective governments.

Absolute rigidity in exchange rate commitments by member countries who are *not* at the same level of economic performance is a recipe for failure. The strength of the EMS lies in its pragmatic flexibility which allows for differences in the economic performances, inflation rates and balance of payments positions of member states by explicitly permitting currency realignments.

THE REASONS WHY THE UK HAS NOT JOINED THE ERM OF THE EMS

The Bank of England pointed to the following factors, in June 1983, which have kept the UK out of the ERM:

1. The UK has had an alternative financial anchor in its firm adherence to a policy of money supply control, as outlined in the UK government's Medium Term Financial Strategy; hence it has not been felt necessary to have a second anchor for sterling in the ERM.
2. Sterling, as a petrocurrency, is particularly exposed to fluctuating pressures, especially those related to oil price movements and expectations. These tend to push sterling in the *opposite* direction from other European currencies, and have made sterling the 'odd man' out of the currencies participating in the ERM.
3. When conditions do become appropriate for sterling's entry into the ERM, then the UK will fully participate in the ERM of the EMS; but that time has not yet come!

However, the House of Lords European Community's Committee concluded, in the autumn of 1983, that the UK should participate in the ERM of the EMS *as soon as possible*, because the UK would then have more influence on the system's development as a full member; this is important both for the UK's more general role within the EEC and also because the EMS is likely to be an important element in attempts to reform the global exchange rate system.

The Confederation of British Industry which, until the buffeting of the pound in the forex markets in 1985, resolutely opposed the UK's entry into the ERM, changed its mind dramatically; it now strongly supports the UK's full commitment to the ERM of EMS. The reasons it gives for the change of heart are as follows:

(a) The credibility of the UK within Europe is being increasingly undermined by the government's refusal to participate in an important part of community policy, viz. the ERM.
(b) The volatility of the exchange rate for sterling would have been averted had sterling been committed to the ERM, at least as regards ERM members, with whom the UK now conducts 44 per cent of its trade.
(c) The major argument which has kept the UK out of the ERM has been that the membership would lead to higher interest rates in order to keep sterling within the prescribed bands; this argument has been undermined, because had the UK been within the prescribed band system of the ERM, it would never have been necessary to raise interest rates in January 1985, by anything like the 4.5 per cent required to deter speculators.
(d) The additon of sterling as an important trading currency would give the ERM still further weight against the US dollar.

It is also worth noting that, despite the monetary targets in the government's Medium Term Financial Strategy, money supply expansion has often overshot the MTFS targets, suggesting that the anchorage of sterling to money supply control targets has not been completely effective.

However, the mere fact of joining the EMS would not make speculators go away. It is far from certain that the central banks have the means or the determination to withstand any major speculative forays between two major traded currencies, e.g. sterling and the deutschmark.

THE RELATIONSHIP BETWEEN INTEREST RATES AND EXCHANGE RATES

Earlier in this chapter, under the portfolio balance theory, it was stated that high interest rates will attract inflows of capital from lower interest rate economies, which in turn will raise the exchange rate of the former. Note that it is changes in the interest rates in a country *relative* to interest rates in other countries, which is the key factor in determining exchange rates.

Interest rates may be raised to reduce outward capital movements and/or to attract capital back. However, the relationship between interest rates and exchange rates extends further. The interest rate is the price of borrowing money, whereas the exchange rate is the price of buying currency. The relationship between interest rate and exchange rate, although indirect, is nonetheless significant in equalizing interest differentials between major international financial centres. This can be shown in the following example.

Suppose a three-month deposit obtained a return of 12 per cent in New York and 10 per cent in London; there is no danger of the dollar depreciating against sterling and there are no exchange controls in either the UK or the USA hindering the free movement of funds between London and New York. The 2 per cent interest differential will encourage UK short-term investors to move sterling from London to New York, and to invest it in overnight US dollar deposits. To do this, they will *sell* sterling and *buy* dollars from their banks at the current (spot) exchange rate between dollar and sterling. This will increase the supply of sterling and increase the demand for the dollar; therefore, on the spot forex market, the *dollar* exchange rate will *appreciate* against sterling. The outflow of sterling will increase its supply, as there will be more sellers than buyers, and will tend to reduce the sterling exchange rate.

If the deposit had been for a longer period, there would be a risk that the dollar may subsequently depreciate against sterling during the three-month period, and that the related capital loss may outweigh the interest rate gain. To cover himself against this outcome, the UK investor could cover his liability *forward*, simultaneously with the original exchange rate transaction. That is, he could buy dollars against sterling spot, and sell dollars against sterling three months forward. The difference between the two exchange rates – spot and forward – is the forward premium (or discount) which will be incorporated in the quotation of forward rates by the UK exchange dealer: the dollar premium will be deducted (and dollar discount added) to the sterling-dollar spot exchange rate. Note that this premium, or discount, must equal the difference between dollar and sterling interest rates, otherwise an 'arbitrage' opportunity will exist.

Thus the corollary of this is that *forward* exchange rates are generally determined by interest rate differentials and not by market expectations.

Arbitrage in the forex markets involves buying and selling currencies to take advantage of exchange rate differentials between currencies. Suppose a London exchange dealer notices that in New York the dollar/sterling rate is being quoted at £1 : $1.11, whereas in London the dollar/sterling rate is £1 : $1.10. He will at once realize that by buying 'cheaper' dollars with pounds in New York and by selling 'dearer' dollars for sterling in London, he will make a quick profit. Thus arbitrage will drive up the dollar/sterling exchange rate quoted in New York and push down the dollar/sterling rate quoted in London; once the exchange rates in the two financial centres equalize, there will be no incentive for arbitrage. The London dealer will, of course, take into account the cost of his buying and selling dollars to decide whether arbitrage is worthwhile. On account of arbitrage opportunities, rates quoted in different financial centres are generally only *slightly* different, but not by enough to trigger arbitrage.

The movement of *long-term* funds between countries will largely depend upon factors such as political stability and the long-term profitability potential of the project which is being financed. Therefore, movements in exchange rate play a less important part in long-term overseas investment decisions.

The relationship between interest rates and exchange rates means that governments can intervene in two ways:

1. by directly buying and selling their currency in the markets;
2. by raising or lowering interest rates.

It may be the latter which has the major impact on their exchange rate.

STERLING EXCHANGE RATE INDEX (SERI)

In times of floating and rapidly moving exchange rates, it can be misleading to focus on the rate of exchange for sterling against any *one* currency. For example, the strength of the US dollar in the early months of 1985 had tended to obscure sterling's relative stability against other currencies. The SERI measures the overall change in the value of sterling against other currencies *as a whole*. SERI therefore is a better indicator of the average exchange rate of sterling, and of the impact of exchange rate movements on UK trade competitiveness or inflation, than is any individual rate such as the dollar/sterling rate. SERI is calculated by taking a weighted average of the sterling exchange rate against 17 other currencies, including the dollar. The weighting reflects the importance of the individual currencies to UK trade. To make it easier to monitor sterling's overall movements, the SERI is calculated and published every hour.

The following six examination questions should give you a good idea of
the breadth and depth of knowledge required to answer questions on
this topic satisfactorily. After you have read this chapter carefully,
spend ten minutes or so making answer plans for each question. Only
then turn to the outline answers given below.

Question 1.

What do you understand by the theory of purchasing power parity?
Discuss the implications of this theory for the operation of the
European Monetary System (EMS).

Question 2.

Discuss both the desirability and the feasibility of a return to worldwide
fixed exchange rates such as operated under the so-called Bretton
Woods system.

Question 3.

Outline the main features of the European Monetary System (EMS).
What do you consider to have been the successes and failures of the
system?

Question 4.

For what reasons and in what ways might the monetary authorities seek
to affect the level of a country's exchange rate?

Question 5.

Following the breakdown of the so-called Bretton Woods system in the
1970s most major currencies were allowed to float. To what extent have
the theoretical advantages of floating exchange rates been borne out in
practice?

Question 6.

Discuss the factors which determine changes in the foreign exchange
rate of a country's currency.

OUTLINE ANSWERS

Answer 1.

Purchasing power parity theory of exchange rates (original form):
- Equilibrium exchange rate between one currency and another
  equalizes domestic purchasing powers of the currencies: if £1 buys
  'x' goods in the UK and $1.10 also buys 'x' goods in the USA, then
  the equilibrium rate must be £1 = $1.10. If not, then goods will be
  imported from the 'cheaper' country, creating a balance of trade
  deficit in the 'dearer' country, whose exchange rate will be
  devalued or depreciated until the equilibrium rate is established.
- Problems with PPP theory (in original form):
  (i)   transport, insurance and other costs ignored;
  (ii) not all goods enter into international trade;
  (iii) relative costs and prices of non-traded goods included in the
        domestic price level, hence comparison of general price
        levels is not reliable in determining exchange rate
        equilibrium.

- PPP theory is particularly relevant in times of differing inflation rates between trading partners; if a country's inflation rate significantly exceeds that of its trading partners, its exports will become less competitive and its imports more competitive, leading to balance of payments problems.
- EMS and PPP theory: EMS attempts to create fixed exchange rates among members. But PPP suggests that as long as members have widely divergent inflation rates, continual realignments of exchange rates to restore price competitiveness will be inevitable; this casts doubt on the durability of EMS. The inflation index at the end of the third quarter of 1982 ranged from 120 (West Germany and Holland) to 180 (Italy and Ireland). In March 1983, the French franc was devalued and the German mark was revalued.

Answer 2.

- Arguments for fixed exchange rates:
    - (i) provide a measure of certainty; favourable to the growth of world trade;
    - (ii) individual countries prevented from pursuing inflationary policies by the need to avoid excessive upward pressure on their exchange rates.
- Arguments against fixed exchange rates:
    - (i) preclude independent domestic policies, requiring deflation rather than devaluation to correct balance of payments deficits;
    - (ii) large holdings of official reserves essential to defend the fixed rate.
- Feasibility of a return to fixed exchange rate system; Bretton Woods system of fixed exchange rates broke down because of:
    - (i) differences in inflation rates;
    - (ii) large imbalances in the balance of payments;

These two factors have increased since the breakdown of Bretton Woods.

Bretton Woods-type exchange rate system unlikely to be durable.

Frequent realignments, even in the 'fixed' exchange rate parities in the EMS, cast doubt on the durability of a fixed exchange rate system.

Answer 3.

- Features of EMS:
    - (i) semi-fixed exchange rate regime for EEC members (except the UK and Greece);
    - (ii) periodic realignments and fluctuations between the currencies within given margins permitted: 2¼ per cent (6 per cent for Italy only) on either side of central rates;
    - (iii) European Currency Unit (ECU), the heart of EMS, is a weighted basket of all EEC currencies (except the drachma); it provides an early warning system of divergences and countries concerned must take action to correct excessive divergences.

- (iv) pooling of 20 per cent of gold and dollar reserves of EEC members, in return for ECU, to support the exchange rate commitments;
- (v) intervention via national currencies; debt settled in ECUs.

- Success of EMS:
  - (i) relative degree of exchange rate stability within EMS since inception in 1979;
  - (ii) has survived eight (four major) realignments – sign of strength;
  - (iii) ECU now approaches a reserve currency status.

- Failures of EMS:
  - (i) Because of different stages of economic development, different inflation rates and balance of payments practices, realignments have been necessary in the past, and will be in the future; but EMS anticipates and allows for realignments at appropriate times.
  - (ii) European Monetary Cooperation Fund – the pool of 20 per cent of national gold and dollar reserves – has not become a fully-fledged European Monetary Fund.
  - (iii) EMS is not an institution, like the IMF, and it has no teeth; member nations must achieve convergence and parity in economic policies and growth.

Answer 4.

- Reasons for seeking to influence the level of exchange rates:
  - (a) Under 'fixed' exchange rate system, the exchange rate must remain at a particular, known level.
  - (b) Under 'floating' exchange rate system, official intervention seeks to smooth sharp movements
    - (i) to improve export competitiveness, via devaluation/ depreciation;
    - (ii) to reduce import bill and domestic inflation rate, via revaluation/appreciation.
- Ways in which exchange rate may be changed:
  - (a) Direct methods:
    - (i) Devaluation/revaluation, under fixed exchange rate system, a la Bretton Woods and EMS.
    - (ii) Direct intervention on the foreign exchange markets.
  - (b) Indirect methods:
    - (i) changes in interest rates: raising interest rates will normally raise or stabilize exchange rate, and *vice versa*.
    - (ii) exchange controls, to limit the purchase of foreign currency.
    - (iii) deflationary policies, to reduce demand for imports.

Answer 5.

- Advantages claimed from floating exchange rates:
  - (i) a continuous and automatic adjustment of the balance of payments.

(ii) independent domestic economic policies can be pursued; no exchange rate target to defend.

(iii) to insulate internal economy from 'imported' inflation; exchange rate moving in line with relative inflation rates. If low relative inflation, balance of payments improves, exchange rate rises and price of imports falls.

(iv) a reduced need for official reserves.

- How far have the theoretical advantages of floating rates actually been achieved?

(i) Automatic adjustment of the balance of payments, especially on current accounts, not a notable success; partly because exchange rates did not move in line with relative inflation rates (purchasing power parity theory), and partly because of low elasticities, at least in the short run. Adjustment of Current and Capital Accounts was not really automatic, but was rather via highly volatile short-term capital flows.

(ii) Although there were no specific exchange rate targets to defend, yet the strength of the US dollar (due to higher interest rates) has constrained the domestic economic policies of other countries.

(iii) Insulation against 'imported' inflation has not been achieved because relative exchange rates have not moved in line with relative inflation rates: low inflation countries (e.g. Germany and Japan) have been most vulnerable to 'imported' inflation.

(iv) 'Free floating' has in fact been 'managed' floating; therefore official interventions have been almost as extensive as under fixed exchange rates, and there is still the need for more official reserves.

(v) The fixed or semi-fixed exchange rate under the EMS means that nine European currencies have **not** been 'floating'.

Answer 6.

Any factors which affect the supply and demand for a currency will affect its exchange rate.

- Factors affecting supply and demand for a currency:

(i) The balance of payments position on current account; a deficit implies less demand and more supply of the currency and therefore lower exchange rates.

(ii) Interest rate differentials; these will affect the level and direction of capital transactions (and thus dividends, profits, interest).

(iii) Inflation rate differentials; these will influence relative cost structures, activate purchasing power parity theory and thus affect current accounts.

(iv) Political stability affects long-term capital flows.

(v) Possession of natural resources, e.g. oil, for which there is inelastic demand overseas.

(vi) Official intervention via exchange controls or intervention on the foreign exchange markets.

(vii) Changes in expectations; 'leads and lags' – traders advance payments in a currency which they expect to appreciate (to avoid capital loss) and delay payments in currencies they expect to depreciate (to make capital gain).

A TUTOR'S ANSWER

Make an answer plan for the following question, which is related to the outline answer 6 above, before looking at the answer plan and specimen answer below.

Question

In the absence of official intervention in the foreign exchange market, what factors are likely to influence changes in a country's exchange rate?

Answer plan
Factors affecting the supply and demand for a currency:
1. The balance of payments position.
2. Relative inflation rates.
3. Relative interest rates.
4. Expectations.
5. The stance of fiscal and monetary policies.
6. Political stability.

Specimen answer

Any factor that can influence the supply of, and demand for, a currency can effect changes in the foreign exchange rate of that currency. The major factors, apart from official intervention, are outlined below, although the strength of each factor varies both between countries and over time.

1. The balance of payments position

A country experiencing a balance of payments surplus on current account will on this count alone experience upward pressure on the exchange rate of its currency; similarly, countries with a current account deficit will tend to experience 'weak' currencies, i.e. a downward pressure on their currencies' exchange rates. Although relative current account performance is widely seen as a key factor in influencing exchange rate movements, the significance of capital account movements should not be overlooked. If, for example, overseas investors have confidence that a country has a considerable development potential and political stability, then they may initiate large-scale capital inflows. These may be sufficient to offset the otherwise downward pressure on its currency of a current account deficit.

2. Relative inflation rates

A country with a high inflation rate relative to its major trading partners will tend to lose competitiveness. This would signal, other things being equal, a deterioration in its balance of payments, which, in turn, will normally cause a fall in the exchange rate of its currency; and vice versa.

3. Relative interest rates	In order to maximize the aggregate returns from his investment portfolio, an investor with a spread of investments in different currencies will seek to ensure that the returns he expects on the marginal investment in different currencies will be approximately equal. By definition, the expected return will be equal to the interest differentials plus the expected change in the exchange rate. Higher interest rates will raise the expected rate of return and lead to a higher demand to invest in the currency offering higher interest rates; this will lead to upward pressure on its exchange rate.
4. Expectations	Foreign exchange markets generally seek to anticipate changes in key economic variables, such as in a country's economic performance and in its level of interest rates. For example, if the markets expect a country's balance of payments to deteriorate, then the exchange rate of its currency may well move downward in anticipation. An expectation of a rise in interest rates for a currency may well move its exchange rate upward. The influence of expectations therefore is of central importance.
5. The stance of fiscal and monetary policy	A government's fiscal and monetary policy stance is seen by the foreign exchange market as a yardstick against which to judge exchange rate behaviour. For example, an increase in money supply, on account of an expansionary fiscal policy, will be seen by many, especially the monetarists, as inevitably leading to a fall in its exchange rate: high money supply growth leads to a high inflation rate and a weak balance of payments position, and hence a weak currency.
6. Political stability	Political stability, or instability, has a very important influence on long-term capital inflows, which will significantly influence the overall balance of payments position, and therefore the exchange rate.

A STEP FURTHER

The factors likely to influence exchange rate movements, under a floating exchange rate system, are assuming ever-increasing importance. Sharp changes in exchange rates are of particular concern to many bank customers and to banks themselves, especially their foreign exchange dealers. Although there is no definitive answer to the problems to which foreign exchange rates – whether fixed, floating or permutations in between – give rise, yet as a prospective banker you are expected to speak intelligently on the broad topic of foreign exchange rates. Try to keep abreast of changes in foreign exchange rates and their effects on the national and international economic scene. You can do this by reading the quality press, *Banking World*, the *Bank of England Quarterly Bulletins* and The Institute of Bankers' *Examiners' Reports* and *Updating Notes*. Pay especial attention to the developments in the EMS; the UK is a member of the EEC and partly involved with the EMS. For a basic understanding of this topic, see the Banking Information Service publication *A Guide to International Financial Systems*.

Chapter 9

International liquidity and eurocurrency markets

- Appreciate the importance of international liquidity.
- Understand the importance and nature of international liquidity.
- Identify and evaluate the types of assets which have served as the basis of world liquidity – gold, national currencies, borrowing facilities, international reserve currencies, SDRs.
- Understand the role of the international banking system, especially in the Euromarkets.
- International Monetary Fund (IMF).
- Appreciate the nature and functions of the eurocurrency markets.
- Understand what is meant by the term 'eurocurrency'.
- Examine the role of the eurocurrency markets in the provision of international finance.
- Appreciate the sources and uses of eurocurrency funds.
- Understand the determinants of the level of eurocurrency interest rates and their inter-relationship with domestic interest rates and exchange rates.

GETTING STARTED

In order to function satisfactorily, an international monetary system should provide for internationally *acceptable* assets in which countries can store their international reserves, and with which they can settle imbalances in their international payments. The concept of 'international liquidity' relates to the degree to which assets are internationally acceptable. At present, in order of importance, the traditional international assets consist of national foreign currency reserves (largely holdings of the US dollar), gold, reserve positions with the International Monetary Fund (the extent to which each member country is able to borrow from the IMF) and Special Drawing Rights (SDRs are internationally acceptable financial assets created by the IMF).

It would, however, be incorrect to view international liquidity purely in terms of traditional holdings of international finance, such as foreign exchange reserves and gold. Another important aspect of international liquidity is the aggregate of internationally acceptable resources *available* to individual countries to finance balance of payments deficits.

To define the term 'eurocurrency market', we need first to define the term 'eurocurrency deposit'. A eurocurrency deposit is simply a deposit taken by a bank in a currency other than the local currency; the bank and the holder of the deposit are outside the control of the central bank which issued the deposit currency. For example, a Eurodollar deposit is a dollar deposit by a US or non-US resident with a US or non-US bank, *so long as the deposit escapes control* by the Federal Reserve Bank of New York.

The international borrowing and lending of eurocurrencies by the international banking system has given rise to the 'eurocurrency markets' (euromarkets). The banks comprising the euromarkets take eurocurrency deposits and make eurocurrency loans to those countries and to others who find it difficult and/or expensive to obtain adequate international finance from traditional sources. The euromarkets have arisen and developed quickly, partly due to the inadequate availability of international liquidity from traditional sources, and partly due to euromarkets being unregulated, so that they are able to offer favourable lending and borrowing terms, i.e. the margin between borrowing and lending is narrow.

ESSENTIAL PRINCIPLES	National currencies circulate freely in settlement of debts within national boundaries because they enjoy general acceptability. There is no equivalent currency that enjoys international acceptability for the settlement of international debts. The lack of an international currency has been a major obstacle to an effective international monetary system.
ASSETS WHICH HAVE SERVED AS THE BASIS OF INTERNATIONAL LIQUIDITY	
Gold	*Gold* performed the functions of an international currency until the 1930s, with the central banks being willing to exchange gold for their national currencies at a fixed rate. However, an ideal international currency would need to grow in line with the needs of international trade and indebtedness. Gold supplies for currency purposes were limited and uncertain; hence it could not be an adequate basis for an international monetary system. It is, however, still an important component of central bank reserves.
US dollar	After the end of the Second World War, the *US dollar*, to a large extent, took on the role of an international currency, because it was

generally acceptable internationally. This acceptability as a means of payment and store of value was due to

(a) the strength of the US economy;
(b) its convertibility into gold;
(c) the fact that the US gold reserves were greater than the US official international debts.

For nearly 25 post-war years, the dollar was the basis of an international currency system. The dollar made up practically the entire foreign exchange reserves of the central banks the world over. The growing demand for the dollar was satisfied by the US government, either by the export of capital or by a deficit on their current account. However, as the US balance of payments deficits began to mount, the dollar failed to hold on to its international currency status. When, in 1971, the US external debts exceeded the US gold reserves, the dollar convertibility into gold was abolished. Soon afterwards, in 1973, it was devalued, not only against gold, but also against some major currencies. The central banks that had held on to their dollars in their foreign exchange reserves suffered sizeable losses in terms of other major currencies. Confidence in the dollar began to wane. This suggests that no national currency, however strong its economy, can continue to function as an international currency for ever.

Special Drawing Rights

Due to the rapid increase in international trade after the war, the shortage of international liquidity was acutely felt, especially during the 1960s. To alleviate this shortage, national governments agreed in 1969, via the IMF, to create an artificial reserve currency: *Special Drawing Rights* (SDRs). Allocations of SDRs were made to IMF member governments in proportion to their subscription to the IMF, which itself is based on the size of their economy and their share in world trade. Deficit countries could borrow foreign currencies from surplus countries in exchange for SDRs; hence the SDRs were given the name 'paper gold'. SDRs have, to a limited extent, alleviated the shortage of international liquidity; by 1982, SDRs 21.3 billion were created and allocated by the IMF. The Second Amendment to the Articles of the IMF in 1978 'demonitized' gold by making regular gold sales and by confirming the SDR as the principal reserve asset of the international monetary system. Yet by 1982 SDRs formed only 6 per cent of the total of national reserve assets. The developed countries have resisted the creation of new SDRs on grounds that this would be inflationary.

While SDRs have been largely unsuccessful as a readily available medium of exchange and as a store of value, they remain important as a unit of account and as a standard for deferred payments: SDRs are used in denominating loans, bonds, grants, etc. and also in the settlement of some financial obligations.

IMF reserve positions

Another source of international liquidity is the *reserve positions of member countries with the IMF*. Each country is required to make a quota subscription. Each country's quota is made up of 75 per cent of its own currency and 25 per cent in SDRs. Any country confronted with a balance of payments deficit can borrow from the IMF foreign currencies up to the value of the SDR component in its quota; this is called its reserve position with the IMF. Although the IMF quotas of members have been increased eight times (by 1985, the total of quotas was SDR 89.2 billion), in terms of the overall reserve compositions of the member countries, reserve positions in the IMF remain of limited importance.

Other foreign currencies

Confronted with demonitized gold, a sliding dollar, lacklustre SDRs and insufficient reserve positions with the IMF, countries have moved towards a *multiple reserve system*; although the dollar still remains the major component, other 'strong' currencies, e.g. German marks, yen, Swiss francs and sterling make sizeable contributions to total reserves.

The official international financial assets which form the basis of international liquidity are, in order of importance, the US dollar, gold, multiple foreign currency reserves, reserve positions in the IMF and SDRs. However, the aggregate of official international financial assets is woefully inadequate to meet the needs of international indebtedness. This inadequacy is one of the principal causes of the rise and rapid development of euromarkets.

THE ORIGIN AND THE RAPID GROWTH OF EUROMARKETS

In this context the London banks were first in the field, and the eurodollar was the vanguard of the eurocurrencies and euromarkets. The eurodollar market had evolved in London to cope with the huge demand for the dollar – it was most widely used to finance international trade, and there was a massive supply of dollars in Europe. The eurodollar market was very profitable because dollars outside the US control were not subject to the low- or no-interest bearing reserve requirements of the US monetary authorities. Therefore, the London and overseas branches of the US and other banks consistently offered higher interest rates on dollar *deposits* than were offered in the USA; and dollar *loans* were often cheaper in London than in New York.

The weakness of the dollar in the 1970s, and the strengthening of other national currencies, gave rise to the euromarkets, borrowing and lending in the deutschmark, Swiss franc, yen and sterling, and to a lesser extent many other currencies, e.g. guilders, French franc. The largest euromarket, apart from the dollar, is in the deutschmark. Any currency which is being deposited and lent in sufficient quantity outside its own country of origin, and which is therefore free of official domestic controls, becomes eurocurrency; and soon a euromarket develops, in that currency. Thus the euromarkets in other currencies emerged for largely the same reason as the eurodollar market: to avoid the expensive reserve requirements of their respective central banks.

The extremely rapid growth of the euromarkets is reflected in the aggregate outstanding lending in all eurocurrencies which reached a peak in 1982 of some $2000 billion. However, the unregulated nature of the market means that this aggregate figure can only be an estimate made by the Bank for International Settlements in Basle, Switzerland.

Since 1982 the growth in eurocurrency lending has fallen, largely as a reaction to the international debt crisis, and also because of the reduction in the current account imbalances of many countries. A further factor responsible for the slowing down of eurocurrency lending by banks has been a marked increase in disintermediation, which has reduced considerably the role of banks as the direct intermediaries between international borrowers and lenders. A host of new financial instruments and techniques have been developed which have widened the scope of borrower and lender alike. The emergence of these securities has fundamentally altered the role of banks as direct intermediaries, although they are major participants in these new areas.

The term 'eurocurrency markets' describes the activities of commercial banks competing for eurocurrency deposits and loans. Business is conducted via telex, telephone and other highly sophisticated and fast means of communication in the major financial centres throughout the world. London is still the principal centre of activity (although New York now runs it a very close second), and that is a major reason why so many overseas banks have established London offices during the last two decades. Other centres are Luxembourg, Paris, Canada, Tokyo, Singapore, Hong Kong, the Middle East and the Caribbean.

THE SOURCE AND USES OF EUROCURRENCY FUNDS

Eurocurrency deposits are usually plentiful since the international banks operating in euromarkets are able to offer stated and higher interest rates on eurocurrency deposits and since eurocurrency depositors, mainly commercial companies, usually prefer to hold currency deposits with banks in their own countries, which then take the form of time deposits.

Banks compete for deposits because they are virtually certain of on-lending funds at a higher rate than they are paying the depositors; these funds go to large commercial companies, governments, publicly-owned bodies and to other banks. In fact, most currency borrowing and lending is inter-bank: banks short of funds in a particular currency borrow from banks with surplus funds of that currency. Inter-bank borrowing and lending is mainly short-term: almost half of deposits and a third of loans are for terms of less than one month.

However, medium-term loans to non-bank borrowers are not uncommon these days: loans for three to eight years account for 20 per cent of total foreign currency lending of British banks. Medium-term loans are largely funded by three and six months' deposits, and banks, in order to protect their profit margins, lend at floating rates, i.e. adjustable to their cost on deposits, usually linked to either the three-month or six-month dollar LIBOR. The dollar and sterling LIBOR are the London eurodollar and the London sterling inter-bank rates respectively. In the case of large loans, e.g. $100 million to a large multinational company, a syndicate of, say, 10 banks may be organized, each bank thus minimizing its risk exposure by providing an agreed portion of the loan.

Large borrowers usually prefer fixed-rate finance to floating-rate finance because they then know the exact cost of borrowing. To meet this preference of large currency borrowers, a *eurobond* market has developed which provides medium-term, fixed-rate finance. The eurobond finance differs from floating-rate finance: with floating-rate loans, banks actually *advance* funds, whereas with eurobonds, banks merely *arrange* the issue and underwriting of bonds, most of which are taken up by private investors. Banks also provide a secondary market in eurobonds, i.e. they buy and sell existing bonds, and thus create liquidity in the eurobond market.

The euromarkets have considerably widened the sources of cheaper and convenient international liquidity for bank and large non-bank borrowers. For example, a UK multinational company which needs dollars and deutschmarks for expansion in the USA and Germany may be able to obtain dollars and deutschmarks on the London euromarket with greater convenience and at cheaper rates than it would pay if it borrowed dollars and deutschmarks in New York and Frankfurt respectively. Therefore the growth of euromarkets has widened competition for deposits, not only to meet the genuine needs of borrowers, but also for arbitrage.

Interest rate differentials in various financial centres, other things being equal, tend towards equilibrium on account of arbitrage: funds flow into centres offering higher rates and away from centres offering lower rates. However, to determine whether arbitrage, via movements of eurodeposits, would be profitable, the cost of covering forward to eliminate the risk of loss occurring due to changes in exchange rates, must be set against the advantage of the interest rate differential. Interest rate differentials must be sufficiently greater than the cost of covering forward, if arbitrage is to take place.

Euromarkets therefore compete for deposits with domestic financial markets in the main countries: this competition has arguably not only increased the general efficiency of domestic financial markets and euromarkets, but also of domestic and international banking.

THE NEED FOR REGULATION OF EUROMARKETS

There are four main problems which arise due to the unregulated nature of euromarkets.

1. Without exchange controls, the flows of a eurocurrency create problems of monetary policy for the monetary authorities whose currency is being used. The unregulated and uncontrolled euromarkets offer deposit and loan facilities in competition with the closely regulated and controlled domestic financial markets. This creates problems for the central banks in restraining money supply to control inflation and expenditure.

   The extent to which euromarkets undermine the effectiveness of national restrictive monetary policy depends upon the type of control used. If quantitative controls (e.g. lending and interest rate ceilings) are used to curb the growth of credit, then there is an incentive for companies to look towards uncontrolled euromarkets.

2. Eurocurrencies flow around the banking system as contra items in banks' balance sheets, rather than flow across the foreign exchanges. These transfers of funds place great pressure not on the central monetary reserves of the eurocurrency centres, but on the banking systems of the countries involved, which could make over-lent banks quite distressed.

3. Banks in most countries are subject to official regulations, which limit their freedom to compete against each other for deposits and loans, for reasons of monetary policy. Banks apply prudential regulations themselves to ensure their own financial soundness and to retain public confidence. However, the same banks have little official control over their euromarket activities, and since several banks have over-lent to borrowers who are now unable to keep repayment dates, it may be argued that international prudential regulations on eurocurrency business have not been sufficiently closely observed. The principles which are adhered to in domestic lending by banks have not been fully adhered to in eurocurrency lending, otherwise several banks which were active in euromarkets would not have collapsed, and several others would not now be caught by the international debt crisis. The international debt crisis has led to requests for the rescheduling of repayment dates from distressed, over-borrowed, less-developed countries, which cannot easily be denied. If a borrower owes his bank £1000, then he is at the mercy of the bank, but if he owes the bank £1 billion, then the bank is at his mercy!

4. The growth of eurocurrency deposits has made foreign exchange rates more volatile and has meant that central banks find it increasingly difficult and expensive to intervene in support of one or other currency. This has led to the concerted action observed in the foreign exchange markets.

The euromarket problem is aggravated by the absence of any known lender of last resort, although in recent years arrangements have been made through the Bank for International Settlements (BIS) for some *ad hoc* support to be activated if needed. The BIS was set up after the First World War to make possible close cooperation between the central banks of European countries. Its headquarters are in Basle, Switzerland, where most governors of European central banks meet once a month to discuss mutual problems.

The phenomenal growth of euromarkets during the past two decades has increased awareness of the importance of effective prudential supervision of banks' international activities. A committee of bank supervisors from ten major industrial countries was set up in 1975, and it agreed certain principles for the supervision of international banking, e.g. the principle of 'parental supervision'. This states that the national banking supervisory authorities are primarily responsible for the supervision of the foreign branches of their countries' banks, but that the supervision of foreign subsidiaries is the responsibility of the two authorities concerned. For example, the prudential supervision of the London branch of a US bank is primarily the responsibility of the US banking supervisory authorities, but the supervision of a British subsidiary of a US bank is the responsibility of both the Bank of England and the US authorities. The BIS now coordinates the supervision of commercial banks operating in many countries through the various central banks concerned.

The ultimate size of euromarkets will be determined by the demand and supply of eurocurrencies, by the relative competitiveness of these markets and the profitability of this type of business. The euromarkets have increased international liquidity and credit and therefore have contributed, to some extent, towards international inflation. They have probably facilitated currency speculation, necessitating difficult and expensive official intervention by the central banks whose currency is the object of speculation; this may have had undesirable monetary repercussions. On the other hand, euromarkets have carried out the vital role of 'recycling' petro-dollars: dollars used to pay for oil to OPEC are deposited by OPEC in short-term euromarket bank deposits, which the banks on-lend, mainly to the less developed countries to pay for their oil imports.

USEFUL APPLIED MATERIALS

THE INTERNATIONAL DEBT CRISIS AND THE IMF

The seeds of the current international debt crisis lay in the hikes in oil prices during the 1970s. Oil has a worldwide and highly inelastic demand. Therefore, the quadrupling of oil prices in 1973 and doubling in 1979/80 by the Organization of Petroleum Exporting Countries (OPEC) had a traumatic worldwide economic and financial impact. The current account surpluses of the OPEC rose to $114 billion in 1980, whereas the deficits of oil-importing industrial and non-industrial countries rose in 1980 to $40 billion and $89 billion respectively. The overall level of imports by the OPEC did increase, but certain Middle Eastern countries with small populations could spend or invest internally only a small fraction of their surpluses. Therefore enormous surpluses in terms of dollars and other major currencies used to pay for their oil exports were available to the OPEC for investment overseas. Currency movements depended upon where the OPEC chose to invest their surpluses: in practice they chose to acquire short-term investments with the commercial banks operating in the euromarkets.

The world was on a floating exchange rate system and, in theory, movements in exchange rates should have eliminated the current account imbalances; but floating rates were unable to achieve equilibrium for two reasons:

1. The surpluses were not utilized to any appreciable extent for imports from or investments in, *non-industrial* oil-importing countries. The balance of payments of such countries received little help from the activities of OPEC.
2. The deficit *industrial* countries which did receive the OPEC short-term deposits found either that their money supply increased alarmingly, if the deposits were in terms of their own currency, or that their exchange rate rose, if the deposits were in

some other currency; a higher exchange rate worsened their normal trading position.

Thus the response in oil-importing countries – non-industrial and industrial – was two-fold: to reduce oil consumption and to apply deflationary policies. The demand for oil is comparatively inelastic to price changes, at least in the short run, and therefore the effect of deflationary policies was to reduce demand for goods and services *other than oil*. This increased domestic unemployment and, to some extent, reduced non-oil imports. Thus deflationary policies tended to transfer one oil-importing country's deficit to other non-oil importing countries.

The industrial countries, through deflationary policies and progress in the development of oil substitutes and oil exploration, have succeeded in eliminating their current account deficits. Unfortunately this has been largely at the expense of the *non-industrial oil-importing countries*, whose exports fell because of the deflationary policies of the industrial countries. This was a significant reason for the debt crisis of the non-industrial oil-importing countries, because the only way they could eliminate their balance of payments deficits, and even then only on a temporary basis, was to take foreign currency loans from any available source; their own foreign currency reserves being hopelessly inadequate to sustain any prolonged deficit.

There was a clear need for recycling the surpluses of OPEC to the deficit oil-importing countries, and even to the other oil-producing countries, such as Mexico, Nigeria and Indonesia, which wanted more foreign exchange to develop their economies. The recycling was done largely by the international banking system, via the euromarkets: this involved the surplus countries depositing some of their surplus funds with major commercial banks operating in euromarkets; the banks then on-lent these eurocurrency deposits to countries in balance of payments difficulties. Thus international banking increasingly took on the role of the IMF, by providing balance of payments finance.

International lending by *commercial banks* to *less developed countries* (LDCs) grew rapidly during the 1970s. There were several reasons for this trend:

(a) the economic recession considerably reduced lending opportunities in the industrialized countries;
(b) there were brighter lending prospects in LDCs, partly because of rising commodity prices;
(c) this form of lending was free from the costs of official regulation for the banks;
(d) there was a belief that countries, unlike private borrowers, would never default on repayments;
(e) the resources of the IMF, the official source of currency funds, were trivial in comparison with the funds at the disposal of commercial banks;

(f) the deficit LDCs preferred to borrow from the international
     banking system rather than from the IMF; borrowing from
     commercial banks was unconditional and cheaper;
(g) margins looked attractive to the commercial banks.

However, the commercial banks and the eurocurrency markets
were not well equipped for the role of lenders of last resort for balance
of payments finance. They had comparatively little experience of
assessing the risks of lending to governments. By the beginning of the
1980s, commercial banks began to sense that they were becoming
overlent, and began to cut back on new lending to LDCs, from $51
billion in 1981 to $25 billion in 1982; this precipitated the international
debt crisis.

Apart from the massive build-up of bank debts to non-oil LDCs,
the specific origins of the international debt crisis of the LDCs, were:

(a) A large portion of bank debt was short-term, of less than one
     year; the LDCs could not meet repayment and servicing dates,
     because oil-induced payment deficits cannot be rectified within
     one year!
(b) Major industrial countries, in order to control rising inflation
     rates, were pursuing fluctuating interest rate policies; higher
     interest costs placed a still heavier burden on the LDCs, forcing
     them to borrow still more.
(c) The worldwide recession meant falling exports of commodities
     and raw materials from the LDCs.
(d) Some of the LDCs were suffering from serious failures of their
     domestic economic policies.

Currently there are 35 countries around the world seeking
rescheduling of their outstanding debts, which amount to some $300
billion. Once the banks suddenly withdrew from additional lending to
LDCs, they were generally unable to pay interest on debts because
they were running huge current account deficits. If they could not
raise new funds, the risk of default and even repudiation was very
serious and this, if it materialized, could have escalated into an
international banking crisis. It is this dangerous situation that has
given new life and importance to the IMF. After several years in the
wings, the IMF has found a key role in the international debt crisis,
i.e. as an intermediary between the international banking system and
the distressed LDCs.

IMF lending to non-oil LDCs in 1982 was a mere $17 billion, and
was grossly inadequate in view of the LDCs' loan commitments of
some $60 billion per annum. Both the IMF and the commercial banks
needed each other to avoid defaults: banks needed the IMF position
to enforce deflationary policies in LDC economies, and the IMF
needed the resources of the banks to help LDCs finance their interim
payments to the Fund.

The solution has been found in a joint system which is by now
well established, and which functions as follows:

1. Through the BIS, the central banks have promised bridging loans to distressed LDCs until they hammer out an agreement with the IMF for long-term assistance.
2. The IMF prescribes a deflationary economic programme; once this is agreed, the IMF releases a standby credit.
3. Simultaneously, those banks which have major exposure to the LDC concerned form an advisory committee. Along with the IMF, they agree a rescheduling of existing debts, and establish a target for new funds.
4. The lead bank in the advisory committee tries to persuade other banks lending to the LDC to release new funds. This is done only along with the rescheduling of existing debts, and after the LDC puts into effect the deflationary programme agreed with the IMF.

The crises among Latin American LDCs is far from over. The stringent economic conditions imposed by the IMF are making economic recovery more difficult for debtor nations.

Despite the success of the scheme from the banks' point of view, and despite meeting the short-term needs of the distressed LDCs, the problem of international liquidity is still there: banks have limited lending capacity, and more and more LDCs are seeking rescheduling and new funds. Large numbers of banks want to disengage themselves from international lending. Should the banks refuse to put up adequate new funds, the joint financing system will come to a halt, unless there is a sharp increase in world economic expansion, a rapid increase in commodity prices and a large increase in the resources at the disposal of the IMF.

Despite a recent increase of about $50 billion in the resources of the IMF (increase in members' quotas – $31.5 billion; expansion of the General Agreement to borrow from the ten largest IMF members plus Switzerland – $12 billion; a bridging loan from the BIS and Saudi Arabia – SDR 6 billion), they are still very inadequate. However, the IMF can borrow from the central banks and from commercial banks. The general view is that if the IMF could borrow up to $10 billion a year from the market it might have sufficient funds to deal with the crisis. However, in this context, the IMF is caught in a cross current of influential opinion. Most governments are pleased with the role that the IMF is playing in negotiating both the rescheduling of debt repayments and new loans; new loans are increasingly conditional upon the distressed LDCs obtaining the IMF guarantee of good housekeeping by implementing the agreed package of deflationary measures in their economies. Nevertheless, governments are hesitant to give the IMF real and long-term powers which might make it too powerful and too independent of them. There is clearly a need for a better balance between official and commercial lending in international finance; this would reduce the risk that a sudden withdrawal of commercial lending (or the failure of some major banks) could precipitate the repudiation of international debt, leading into a fully-fledged international banking crisis.

LENDING FACILITIES PROVIDED BY THE IMF	One of the objectives of the IMF is to provide financial suport to member states suffering with *temporary* balance of payments deficits. It provides this type of financial support via several facilities.
The reserve tranche	Members of the IMF deposit an official quota to the IMF funds, made up of national currencies (75 per cent) and, until 1976, of gold (25 per cent). Since 1976, gold has been replaced with SDRs (25 per cent). A member can borrow up to 25 per cent of its quota, known as the gold or reserve tranche, automatically and without IMF conditions.
Credit tranche	If the country concerned still needs further assistance, it can obtain four credit tranches from the IMF; these are denominated in the required currencies, and each tranche is equal to 25 per cent of the country's quota. However, each tranche carries progressively more stringent IMF conditions on the economic policy to be followed by the borrower.
	The IMF currency lending under the reserve and credit tranche is against a deposit of equal value in the borrowing country's own currency. A member country may only borrow the currencies it needs to meet its temporary balance of payments deficit, up to 125 per cent of its quota. This is because the IMF will not hold more than 200 per cent of a country's quota in that country's currency (and it already holds 75 per cent!). Borrowings under the reserve tranche will be credited to the country's foreign currency reserves, which are used to support the exchange rate of the domestic currency. The loans under the credit tranches will be used for official financing of the balance of payments deficit.
Compensatory financing facility	This lending facility was introduced in 1963 to 'compensate' for a temporary fall in export earnings largely due to natural disasters, such as floods or crop failures.
Supplementary financing facility	This facility was devised in 1979 to assist 'developing countries' facing serious balance of payments deficits due to the massive increases in oil prices. This facility was meant to supplement a distressed country's credit tranche, so that it was enabled to borrow, under 'hard' IMF conditions, in excess of its quota and for longer periods. Resources for the facility were provided by some surplus fund members and institutions. The loans are normally given by the IMF under standby arrangements: the borrower agrees an economic programme with the IMF, performance targets are set and more funds are released by the Fund as the borrower achieves more of the performance targets.
Extended credit facility	Normally a borrowing country is required to 'repurchase' its drawings from the IMF through buying back its own currency with other currencies. However, under this facility, the country is given a longer repurchase period – in some cases up to 10 years – during which to adjust its economy.

Bufferstock facility	Finance is made available to primary commodity producers under this facility to build up bufferstocks at times of falling world prices; these may help prevent undue price fluctuations and help stabilize the export earnings of commodity producers.
Enlarged access facility	This facility assists countries with large deficits relative to their quotas; a country may borrow up to 150 per cent of its quota in a year. Saudi Arabia, Switzerland and the BIS mainly provided resources to fund this IMF facility.
General agreement to borrow	This is an important but exclusive club of the ten rich countries, who have agreed to provide additional funds to the IMF, which can be borrowed by any member of the Group of Ten. The above arrangements are designed to assist member states to rectify temporary balance of payments deficits without changes in exchange rates. However, despite increases in members' quotas, IMF resources via the sales proceeds from gold auctions and additional borrowing, have been inadequate relative to the needs of member countries in balance of payments difficulties. The inadequacy of the Fund's resources has been partly alleviated by the extra lending of the euromarkets.
THE SPECIAL DRAWING RIGHTS (SDRs) OF THE IMF	The IMF, in an attempt to generate additional international liquidity, created a new composite reserve currency, called the SDR, in 1969 (see the 'Specimen Answer' below). Although the total of SDRs to be created was at the discretion of the IMF, their allocation among members was strictly in proportion to members' quotas. SDRs do not exist physically; there are no SDR bank notes. They are book entries in the accounts of member countries with the IMF. Transfer entries are made in settlement of debts between countries. Every effort has been made to get the SDR internationally accepted as the main reserve asset.

(a) It was initially valued in terms of gold to make it acceptable as a world currency.
(b) The Jamaica Agreement (1976) implemented in 1978, 'legitimized' floating exchange rates under the supervision of the IMF, and demonetized gold, in order to reduce its status, and to raise the status of the SDR as a reserve currency.

The Second Amendment to the IMF Articles effected by the Jamaica Agreement, not only stated that the SDR should become the principal reserve asset of the international reserve system, but also permitted the direct use of the SDR to be extended; e.g. for forward operations, making loans, settlement of financial obligations, donations and grants, and for currency swap and spot transactions. The IMF was also allowed to extend the number of users of SDRs beyond the member countries, and into international institutions, such as the BIS.

(c) The SDR ceased to be valued in terms of gold, but was valued in terms of a basket of 16 major currencies; this was to increase the confidence in, and international acceptance of, SDRs as reserve assets. In 1981, the SDR was valued in terms of five major currencies, US dollar, deutschmark, sterling, French franc and yen, to give it still greater credibility.

Despite these attempts to make SDRs the principal international reserve asset, it has largely not been accepted as such. It is, however, more acceptable as unit of account and standard of deferred payments. As a composite currency, it is relatively stable in value against the major reserve currencies, so much so that a number of countries peg their exchange rate to the SDR.

There are two main reasons why the SDR has failed to become the principal reserve store of value:

1. The resistance by the developed countries to the creation of new SDRs, on the grounds that additional SDRs wil be inflationary.
2. The fact that the world has remained more enamoured of gold and foreign currencies, in preference to SDRs, as reserve assets.

THE SECOND AMENDMENT TO THE ARTICLES OF THE IMF

This amendment, based on the Jamaica Agreement (1976), came into effect in 1978. In addition to upgrading the position of the SDR (and downgrading gold) as the principal reserve asset, the amendment 'legitimized' floating exchange rates but with the following proviso:

(a) If 85 per cent of the membership agreed, then the full membership of the IMF would return to an 'adjustable peg' par value system, with permitted fluctuation of 2¼ per cent ($\pm$) around par values. However, until a return to the par value system, floating exchange rates would continue and would be monitored by the IMF.
(b) Any member country, with the approval of the IMF, may relinquish the par value system and adopt a floating exchange rate.

EUROPEAN CURRENCY UNIT (ECU) OF THE EMS

ECU is based upon a basket of all the currencies in the EEC. It includes sterling and the drachma even though the UK and Greece have remained outside the EMS.

The weight of each currency in the basket is allocated on the basis of the EMS central rates, so that it shifts when the central rates are adjusted. Each currency unit must vary in weight according to its rise and fall in value compared to other currencies in the basket.

The ECU has a powerful attraction for citizens of countries with weak currencies. These include currencies which have been devalued in the past, or are likely to be devalued in the future, e.g. the currencies of Belgium, France and Italy. By denominating deals in ECUs, buyers are increasingly availing themselves of the protection offered by an ECU against the down-grading of their own national currencies. This is because the spread of the basket over a number of stronger currencies means that the dramatic changes which occasionally occur between two currencies are spread out over all the currencies in the basket. This also means that those countries with strong currencies do not have any great incentive for going into ECU denominated investments. For instance, in Germany, ECU issues are not authorized. On the other hand, countries with weak currencies greatly benefit from ECU-linkage. For example, Italy has authorized the use of ECU's as an official foreign currency, and up to 20 per cent of Italian export invoicing is in ECU.

The ECU has been one of the main beneficiaries of the massive exchange rate swings and interest rate fluctuations, in recent years. For instance, firms with subsidiaries in several EEC countries can avoid the problem of dealing in several different currencies by using ECUs. Due to its relative stability against most EEC currencies, it has been used increasingly by business companies as a hedging instrument against foreign exchange fluctuations. In 1983, there were 1.5 billion ECU-denominated eurobonds. The ECU is gaining in importance and its use will continue to increase. Some knowledge of the ECU for those living in rural areas of the UK will be of particular relevance, since the EEC is likely to pay support payments to farmers in the ECU in future.

EUROCURRENCY INTEREST RATES

Eurocurrency rates are prices of currencies outside the jurisdiction of their respective national central banks; the prices in euromarkets are, like all prices in near perfect markets, determined by the supply (eurocurrency deposits) and demand (eurocurrency loans) for eurocurrency funds. The rates thus determined appear to be attractive to both borrowers and lenders, otherwise the eurocurrency markets would not have grown to the extent that they have done.

The UK banks do lend sterling to overseas residents, but much international lending is eurocurrency lending. Therefore the euro interest rates must be fairly competitive with domestic interest rates. Suppose the domestic interest rates in Germany rose above the eurodeutschmark rate in London, then the eurodeutschmark rate will quickly rise to a competitive level to stop eurodeutschmark deposits flowing back to Germany to take advantage of the higher domestic deutschmark rates. Thus the relationship between the euro interest rates and domestic interest rates is such as to keep them both at the same level. Of course this relationship need not hold if there are exchange controls in operation preventing the free flow of currencies; consequently, in these circumstances, euro and domestic rates may differ quite substantially.

The following example shows the relationship between euro rates and exchange rates. Suppose the exchange rate of the deutschmark appreciated against sterling from, say £1 = DM3.75 to £1 = DM3.00. A customer of a UK bank holding deutschmark deposits might find it profitable to sell his deutschmarks and buy cheaper sterling, and invest the sterling proceeds into sterling deposits at sterling deposit rates. To prevent this happening, the bank will have to increase the interest paid on deutschmark deposits to reflect the appreciation in the exchange rate of the deutschmark against sterling.

The difference between the spot (current) and forward rates generally reflects the differences between the eurodeposit rates between two currencies. Euromarkets are borrowing and lending markets, and swap agreements between banks are frequent. Suppose Bank X has eurodeutschmark funds and Bank Y has eurodollar funds; the eurodollar rate is 6 per cent per annum, and the eurodeutschmark rate is 5.5 per cent per annum, and the exchange rate between these two eurocurrencies is $1 : DM3. A swap arrangement between X and Y would operate something like this: X buys, say, $100,000 from Y for DM300,000, and at the same time agrees to buy back DM300,000 for $100,000 after one year. Under this swap agreement X will gain 0.5 per cent and Y will lose 0.5 per cent on interest rate differentials between dollars and deutschmarks. Clearly Y will not agree to be a party to this swap agreement without some compensation for the loss of 0.5 per cent interest. However, the compensation comes from the difference between the spot and forward rates: the forward dollar spot rate will buy a premium margin of 0.5 per cent per annum. Due to the differential between spot and forward rates of the dollar, both X and Y would earn the same amount of interest as they would have done with their original currencies had they not swapped, because the swap agreement, seen from Y's viewpoint, will mean that a forward discount margin will apply to his deutschmarks. Forward margins of premium and discount are completely interwoven, and it is the difference between eurocurrency deposit rates that determine the forward discount and premium margins: the larger the eurorate differential, the bigger the forward margins of premium and discount, and vice versa. Therefore the forward exchange rate does not necessarily equal the market's expectation of where the exchange rate is going.

RECENT EXAMINATION QUESTIONS	The following six recent examination questions on the two topics of 'international liquidity' and 'eurocurrency markets' show the relationship between these two areas of the Monetary Economics syllabus. Prepare outline answers to these questions before looking at the outline answers given below.
Question 1.	What do you understand by the concept of international liquidity? Assess the importance of the International Monetary Fund (IMF) in ensuring an adequate supply of international liquidity in recent years.
Question 2.	What factors have contributed to the rapid growth of the eurocurrency markets in recent years? To what extent has this growth been a cause of concern to the world's monetary authorities?

Question 3.	What is a eurodollar? Why are changes in eurodollar interest rates of importance to the foreign exchange markets?
Question 4.	(a) Outline the main changes that have occurred in the composition of international liquidity since 1971. (b) To what extent has the existence of floating exchange rates reduced the need for international liquidity?
Question 5.	For what reasons are rates of interest paid on deposits in the euromarkets usually higher than comparable rates paid on domestic deposits? How far does this factor explain the rapid growth in the euromarkets?
Question 6.	What problems have been posed for international liquidity requirements by the large balance of payments surpluses accruing to the oil-producing countries in recent years? To what extent have the Eurocurrency markets helped in overcoming these problems?

OUTLINE ANSWERS

Answer 1.	International liquidity comprises those assets which are internationally *acceptable* in the settlement of debts: foreign exchange reserves (mainly US dollars), gold, reserve positions in the IMF, SDRs.
	● Two-fold role of the IMF:
	  (i) Adding to total international liquidity – relatively small; SDR holdings and reserve positions in the IMF significantly less important than holdings of gold and foreign exchange reserves.
	  (ii) Facilitating the pooling and channelling of international liquidity – through its various supplementary financing schemes, the IMF has supplemented the liquidity needs of countries in balance of payments deficits, but these facilities are significantly less than borrowings from the international banking system.
	● IMF has assumed greater importance in recent years due to the overlending by private banks and the overborrowing by some LDCs.
	● IMF conditionality (deflationary policies) now a prerequisite for further loans or rescheduling of existing loans by private banks.
	● IMF's own resources inadequate; call for increasing its resources.
	● IMF's conditionality gives it indirect influence upon the huge liquidity of the private banks.

Answer 2.	Reasons for the rapid expansion of international banking in euromarkets:

- Increase in international banking activity due to growth in world trade and to general internationalization of the world economy; large balance of payments imbalances – surpluses channelled to deficit countries via international banking (in preference to IMF machinery, due to restrictions); euromarkets are unregulated and without costly restrictions (no reserve requirements, etc.), hence can offer favourable lending and borrowing terms.
- Growth in euromarkets has slowed dramatically due to world recession and heavy indebtedness of Less Developed Countries.
- Lack of regulation of euromarkets has led to problems, e.g. the extent of mismatching of lending and borrowing, capital inadequacy, etc.
- Rapid growth in euromarkets leads to rapid growth in international liquidity, hence the concern about the possible inflationary effects.
- A vast pool of 'hot' money in euromarkets potentially destabilizes both exchange rates and domestic monetary policies.

Note: The main point is the lack of restriction, which has been at the heart of all these other growth factors.

Answer 3.

A eurodollar is a dollar deposit held by a US or non-US resident with a bank outside the USA, so long as the deposit escapes the 'jurisdiction' of the Federal Reserve Bank of New York.

- Importance of changes in eurodollar interest rates: *ceteris paribus*.
  - (i) An increase in rates will put upward pressure on the spot dollar exchange rate (because relative international interest rates are a key determinant of exchange rate movements).
  - (ii) An increase will widen the forward discount, or narrow the premium, on the dollar exchange rate (see pp. 165 and 166).
  - (iii) A decrease in eurodollar interest rates will have the reverse effect.

Answer 4.

(a) International liquidity is the aggregate of the resources available to individual countries to finance their balance of payments deficits.
- Before the devaluation of the US dollar in 1971, international liquidity comprised dollars, gold, reserve position with the IMF, SDRs, in that order of importance.
- The changes since the dollar devaluation:
  - (i) The 'demonitization' of gold by the US and the IMF, but increase in its importance until 1981, due to increase in gold market prices; in recent years gold prices have fallen rapidly, but gold is still a favoured component of international liquidity.
  - (ii) The US dollar is the major currency in the foreign exchange reserves, but a 'diversification' in the various countries' exchange reserves has led to a multiple reserve currency system.

(iii) An expansion in the role of SDRs, but SDRs remain of limited importance in terms of total international liquidity.

(iv) Although the IMF quotas of members have been increased, yet these, in terms of the overall reserve positions, remain of limited importance.

(v) The significant role of eurocurrency markets (international banking system) in supplementing international liquidity.

(b) According to the theory of 'floating' rates, balance of payments imbalances should be self-correcting, thus reducing the need for international liquidity.

- In reality, the need for international liquidity has increased because
  (i) the floating has been 'dirty', and
  (ii) balance of payments' imbalances have become larger because of massive OPEC surpluses.

Answer 5.

- The technical reasons for higher interest rates paid on euromarket deposits:
  (i) the eurocurrency market is unregulated;
  (ii) the absence of reserve requirements lowers the effective costs of these deposits and enables the international banking system to offer higher returns;
  (iii) the existence of exchange controls or regulated domestic banking systems often prevents the free flow of deposits from the domestic market to the euromarket.
- Higher deposit rates and lower lending rates (because of the absence of the cost of reserve requirements) are the two major determinants of the level of the eurocurrency rates, and therefore the major explanation of the rapid growth of euromarkets.

Answer 6.

The concept of international liquidity may be viewed from various aspects; it is wrong to view it purely in terms of traditional sources of international finance.

- The huge OPEC surpluses have been reflected in the large deficits of other countries.
- The continuing large deficits have posed problems of international liquidity.
- For many deficit countries, their official reserves and traditional sources of finance – gold, SDRs, IMF quotas – have been inadequate, thus suggesting a shortage of international liquidity.
- These countries have been able to supplement their international liquidity by borrowing (cheaply and without conditions) from the euromarkets to overcome their short-term liquidity problems.
- The international banking system has attracted huge OPEC eurocurrency deposits (by being able to offer higher returns) and has recycled its deposits to supplement the liquidity shortage of deficit LDCs.

- In alleviating the shortage of international liquidity, the international banking system has created for itself considerable international debt payment problems.
- Even the eurocurrency market resources may be inadequate to deal with the international debt problem.

A TUTOR'S ANSWER

The following recent examination question seeks to test your knowledge of the major international liquidity assets of the international monetary system. Prepare a brief outline plan of your answer to the question, and then write according to that plan, so that you answer the question, the whole question and nothing but the question. Then compare your answer with the answer given below.

Question

Assess the present role in the international monetary system of:

(a) gold;
(b) special drawing rights (SDRs);
(c) the US dollar.

Answer plan
(i) Define international monetary system (briefly).
(ii) Balance the 'past' and the 'present' of the three reserve assets.
(iii) Give prominence to the 'present' position.

Specimen answer

An international monetary system should provide for three things: a generally acceptable way of valuing national currencies against each other; assets in which countries can store their international resources; and a means by which countries can settle their debts with each other.

Gold, SDRs and the US dollars are three assets in which countries may store their international reserves.

(a) Gold.

The central feature of the Bretton Woods agreement was twofold – the exchange rates of the national currencies were pegged against the US dollar, and the dollar was convertible into gold. However, due to the weakness of the dollar, following adverse trends in the US balance of payments, the dollar was devalued twice, before being allowed to float in early 1973. This led to the suspension by the US government of the dollar–gold convertibility. Officially gold was 'demonetized' in the 1976 Jamaica agreement, and by the IMF Second Amendment in 1978. The demonitization of gold implied the official downgrading of gold as a component of international liquidity. It also meant that the official price of gold – $38 an ounce – was abolished. Member countries of the IMF were no longer allowed to use gold as a part of their IMF subscription quotas, and to keep down the market price of gold, the USA and the IMF auctioned gold openly several times. The IMF gold sales were further testimony to the reduced official importance attached to gold in the international monetary system.

Nevertheless, despite the fall in gold prices since 1980, gold still accounts for a substantial percentage of official reserves of countries. Moreover, EMS arrangements require member countries to place 20 per cent of their gold and dollar reserves with the European Monetary Cooperation Fund, in exchange for European Currency Units. Apart from the EMS requirement, there are no central bank transactions in gold, although gold reserves are used as collateral security by countries borrowing currencies. There are also gold 'swap' transactions, i.e. countries selling gold for foreign currencies on condition that they will buy gold back at an agreed price in terms of the currency borrowed.

(b) SDRs.

The IMF attempted to generate additional international liquidity through the creation of an entirely new reserve asset, called the Special Drawing Right. SDRs were first credited to every member country of the IMF in proportion to the size of its subscription to the IMF. A country facing a balance of payments deficit could borrow foreign currencies from surplus countries in exchange for its SDR allocation. These transactions increased international liquidity in the international monetary system in exactly the same way as a bank increases domestic liquidity by lending its depositors' funds. In the first 11 years of their existence, the participant countries have used SDR 33 billion in transactions.

Although the Second Amendment to the IMF Articles in 1978 confirmed SDR as the principal reserve asset in the international monetary system, yet the SDRs formed only about 6 per cent of the total national reserves in 1982. The reason why the SDRs remain the small change of the international monetary system is partly the resistance by the developed countries to the creation of the new SDRs (until January 1981, SDR 21.4 billion were created by the IMF), on the grounds that additional SDRs will be inflationary; and partly because countries have remained more enamoured of gold and foreign currencies as reserve assets. Thus the SDR performs only as a limited means of exchange and store of value function in the system.

SDRs, however, are more important as a unit of account and as a standard of deferred payments: SDRs are used, not only by the participating countries, but also by certain international institutions (such as the Bank for International Settlements, the World Bank) in the settlement of financial obligations, swap arrangements, SDR-denominated forward options, loans and grants and as security in transfer-retransfer agreements. As a 'basket' currency, the SDRs are relatively stable in value against major world currencies and therefore a number of countries peg their exchange rate to the SDR.

(c) The US dollar.

Until the 1970s, the international monetary system was based on a currency reserve system, in which the US dollar was the principal international medium of exchange and store of value. This was because the dollar was convertible into gold, generally acceptable in international payments and was convenient and plentiful in supply; the growing demand for the dollar was satisfied by the US government, either by the export of capital or by a deficit on its current account. Therefore the central banks held a major proportion of their foreign reserves in dollars.

However, confidence in the dollar began to slip when in August 1971 it was devalued, not only against gold but also against some major currencies. The dollar slide between 1971 and 1979 caused the central banks to reduce the dollar content of their foreign reserves and to acquire a wider range of currencies. The multiple reserve currency system did not become popular. Attempts to promote the use of 'strong' currencies such as the German mark, Swiss franc and Japanese yen as reserve currencies were not welcomed by the national governments of these currencies.

For the past few years, the US government has pursued a policy of deficit financing to achieve a higher economic growth and employment level; the deficit has been financed by a policy of high interest rates, which has increased greatly the demand for the dollar. At present, the dollar is the most important reserve currency and retains a dominant position in overall liquidity. The dollar is also dominant as a unit of account in international official and commercial transactions. Many commodities in international trade, e.g. oil and coffee, are priced in terms of dollars. It continues to act as a medium of exchange for much of world trade. Due to the importance of the dollar, many currencies have pegged their exchange rate to it, and movements in dollar exchange rates are therefore of vital importance to many economies.

A STEP FURTHER

The important thing to remember with regard to international liquidity is that any national currency, composite currency or any other commodity will become a legitimate component of international liquidity provided it enjoys international acceptability in debt settlements and investments. With the passage of time, and with changes in international circumstances, certain components of international liquidity become less important and others more important. Observe carefully the development of the up and coming ECU. You should also continue to to keep an eye open for changes in the UK's position in connection with the ERM of the EMS.

With regard to the euromarkets: they are the products of their time; they evolved because there was need for them and because conditions favoured their development; but their unregulated nature is cause for serious concern. It has led to international debt and banking crises, in which there are several distressed, overborrowed countries and distressed, overlent banks: if these crises are not resolved, either by the international banks on their own, or in partnership with the IMF – which has assumed an important intermediary role – the consequences of failure will be catastrophic.

To keep abreast of changes in this area of the Monetary Economics syllabus, you should study: the *Bank of England Quarterly*

Bulletins, Finance and Development, a quarterly publication of the IMF and the World Bank, *Banking World*, The Institute of Bankers *Examiners' Reports* and *Updating Notes*. The excellent BIS publication, *A Guide to the International Monetary Systems*, will give a good understanding of the fundamentals of international liquidity and eurocurrency markets.

Index